Spiritual Poetry Library Series

Volume Two

Revelation Insight Publishing Co.

© 2010

Dear Reader

1 Corinthians 2, 7-15: We speak the hidden mystical wisdom of God, which God ordained before the world unto our Glory; which none of the princes of this world knew, for had they known it, they would not have crucified the Lord of Glory. However, as it is written, eye has not seen, nor ear heard, neither has it entered into the Heart of man to conceive the things which God has prepared for them that Love him. However, God has revealed them unto us by His Spirit: For the Spirit searches all things, yes, and the deep things of God. For what man knows the things of a man, save the spirit o a man, which is in him? Even so, the thing of God knows no man, but the Spirit of God. Now we have received, not the Spirit of this world, but the Spirit, which is of God; that we might know the things that are freely given us of God. Which things also we speak, not in the words which man's wisdom teaches, but which the Holy Spirit teaches, comparing spiritual things with Spiritual. However, the natural man receives not the things of the Spirit of God. For they are foolishness unto him, neither can he know them, because they are spiritually discerned. Nevertheless, he that is spiritual judges or discerns all things.

Liturgical Poetry

of

Adam of St Victor

The Complete Unabridged Texts

Re-edited for Today's Reader

Behold I stand at the door and knock, if anyone hears my voice and opens the door; I will come in and dine with him, and he with Me. He who overcomes, I will grant to sit down with Me on My throne, as I also overcame and with My Father on His throne. " Rev 3: 20-21

All rights reserved. No part of this book may be reproduced or transmitted in any form or means, electronic or mechanical including photocopying, or by any information storage and retrieval system without permission in writing from Revelation Insight.

ISBN # 978-1-936392-03-2

Library of Congress Cataloging in Publication Data.

#2010929280

BAISAC # REL012120

Printed and bound in the USA

Revelation – Insight © 2010

E Mail: Mystic@Orthodox.com

General Introduction

These are designed and presented to accent a fine library of the essentials required for further in depth investigation of this genre.

The focus of this series is to provide today's reader with the essentials of background and investigative writings that are a part of our Christian heritage. The selected written works are a culmination of screening the best of this genre from the numerous documents, which are available. We selected these works based on a number of factors. The greatest impact upon the body of Christ, their insight of the genre and their related impact on other writers and the feasibility of this text to be used as a guide, in a standalone application. They are the primary indicators used, coupled with other factors in making our selection.

Each text in this series is a premier stand-alone text in this genre. The intended corpus of works pooled together make for a reference library rivaling that of some great monastery or university library on this subject. These are re-edited for today's reader. These writings are not abridged, they are the complete text, completely redone in grammar, syntax, verbiage, and other literary components to ensure the spirit of these works are not lost in these important changes.

For many of these texts, this is the first time they are available in this format and to these standards. These are not a scholarly reference work edition. For that purpose, there are other publications available. This series is intended for those who have a fundamental familiarity with the subject, and some of the writers. The intent is to address the needs of the readers who are journeying forward on their quest in union with God. There are other selections to be added as certain texts are processed. Please look forward to these great works in print, audio and E-book formats at your local bookstore, although us directly.

Spiritual Poetry Series Forward

The staff at "Revelation-Insight" presents this series. The objective of this particular series is to provide the focused reader, student, and others who have a need to go beyond the fundamental basics and achieve something more. This series was designed to provide you with the necessary tools by Thomas Aquinas to have a ready answer to foundational subject matter and answers to key and essential portions of various philosophical and theological works.

These tools will come in the form of apologies, a historical reference, systematic theology and various dissertations. This particular work, which is more than an overview of the accumulative life's effort and its varied formularies; it is an insightful guide. Presenting you with the essential and fundamental key elements required in answering a bevy of questions and perhaps summarizing the information with a need for a deeper explanation.

Throughout this series, there will be additions, which could be considered not simply a reference work but much more, and indeed that is our aim. By, providing you with much more than you intended upon receiving and yet not to the point of becoming overwhelmed. This is our pledge to you the consumer, to always bring to you in a palatable formula and format. To the student, a ready reference, to the reader, to educate through pertinent information, to the educator an essential reference tool for all avenues and venues. This is what we inspire to become for you the consumer. Many times libraries have bits and pieces spread across numerous volumes, requiring numerous hours to comb through. This series is designed and produced to provide you with the correct and proper information you need to come to grasp and obtain a sure foundation in your understanding your history belief events, leading up to its current formulary. Since history is what it is, and the facts remain self evident, in this series, we will not subscribe nor slant our presentations, following particular denominations. We will present these as straightforward as numbers are in a math equation. The rational is the numbers and the equation is what it is. There is no need to interpret. There is only one way to solve, one way to proceed, and only one correct answer to grasp.

Editor's Notes

Rational, Method and Aim of This Modernization

The intention of this book is not for the scholar. Instead, it is for the pilgrim who does not have access, to such works. It is for such individuals, that this edition has been prepared. My aim has been to make Adam of St Victor's meaning clear to the modern reader with as little alteration of the available texts as possible. I have modernized the spelling, have simplified long and involved constructions, and have tried to illuminate the meaning by careful punctuation. I have dealt sparingly with the vocabulary, striving to keep some of the words likely to be understood.

I am aware that by my modernization, I have laid myself open to criticism in many directions. I strove for consistency, and tried solely to retain as far as possible the simplicity and charm of the original spirit and intent

I have dismissed most of the Latin verbiage and some notes.

I have retained the "King's English" in the rhyme.

<u>This text is presented in its entirety. It remains unabridged.</u>

FROM THE TEXT OF GAUTIER,

WITH TRANSLATIONS INTO ENGLISH IN THE

DIGBY S. WRANGHAM, M.A.,

ST. John's College, oxford,

Vicar of Darrington, Yorkshire.

Original Preface

In offering this work to the public I am breaking what is practically new ground to the great majority of English readers. The circumstances, detailed in the introduction to M. Gautier's Edition, of which the larger part of the poetry of Adam of St. Victor was entirely lost to the world for many years after the French Revolution. In this day and age, it appears to be a great to give an interest and novelty regarding it in this country at this day from the only other English Edition, published in Paris in 1858- 9, has only to a very limited degree been averted. I feel therefore that, so far as the original text is concerned, I am doing a good service to the lovers of Medieval Hymnology, by rendering it more accessible to them in this, by using the first edition of it, published in England, and reviving it before it enters into obscurity.

Now regarding what forms the principal part of my work in these volumes, viz., the translations, I feel, on the other hand, that a great apology is due for the imperfections with which I know they abound, and I am anxious therefore to explain the principles, which have guided me in my attempts for they are no better than attempts to render the original into our language.

I have looked at the duty of a translator as equivalent to that of an engraver, and felt that, the poet being a "word painter" the translator must be a "word engraver;" in other words that to be successful, he must reproduce faithfully, as a whole and in detail, what he sets himself to copy. A so called translation, which is stripped at the taste of the translator not only of the form of the original, viz., its meter, but more or less also of the thoughts and expressions with which that form is clothed, appears to me to fail to be what it professes to be, just in proportion as these defects, if I may venture to call them so, appear in it. It may be a very beautiful piece of poetry in itself, and it very often is so, but a translation, i.e., a transferring of a given original from one language into another it can scarcely be.

If I were to take the picture of a beautiful boy with curling locks and "fair and of a muddy countenance," and draw another, as fancy led me, of that same boy in later life, bronzed in the battle of life, of an athletic form and with a flowing beard, although I might keep the pleasing features of the original face before me constantly and reproduce their outline carefully, no one could say that I had made a copy of the picture I had seen.

Those who saw the two portraits together might detect that the child was the father of the man, but that would be all. They would count the two as separate works of are, standing or falling by their own several faults or merits, and never dream that the second was intended to reproduce the first.

What is true of the copyist would seem to be necessarily still truer of the engraver, who has not the help of colors to aid his efforts, as the former has, and is compelled therefore to follow most closely his original both in outline and detail, if he would have that original recognizable at all in the somber hues of his engraving.

In like manner the translator, so far from needing the originality with which some would have him endowed, must be content, I submit, like the engraver, to follow his original painfully, line after line, and not be satisfied with his work till he has succeeded in so reconstructing it, as to leave no doubt upon the mind of the reader of the two works as to their inter identity. In a certain sense, no doubt, an engraver should be an artist, that is to say, he should have a good eye for proportion, and be well versed in the rules of drawing generally; and in the same sense a translator should be something of a poet, with a good ear for rhythm, of proportion of poetry, and not ignorant of the rules of poetical composition. Yet neither engraver nor translator needs to be original, to my mind; for, when his originality comes in at the window, his original goes out at the door. It is a singular fact, for I think it is a fact, that great poets have not been very successful translators, nor successful translators, very great poets. Exceptions there may have been to this rule, but very rare ones. The only great poet who was I can scarcely say a great, but a good translator, that I can call to mind, was Dryden, and his translations are of the freest; while the merits of Milton, Pope, Cowper, Shelley and Keble, as translators, pale before those of Gilford, Neale, Fi'ere and Conington.

Should I seem to go too far were I to suggest that the object of a translator and that of a parodist should be much the same in kind, however different in effect? The difference between them appears to me to be simply this, viz., that, while both preserve the meter of their original, the translator changes its language, and preserves, as far as possible, its meaning, and the parodist changes its meaning, and, as far as possible, preserves its language.

If in these principles, which I cannot help thinking should govern translators, I am at all right, however imperfect may be, and are, my own attempts to carry them out, I need scarcely point out how absolutely essential it is to observe them in translating such an author as Adam of St. Victor, because it is "manner" and not "matter" that is his distinguishing characteristic. Adam's range is not great;" and, therefore, if you take away his meters, which are ever changing even in the same sequence, and his peculiar mode of building them up, until he finishes with a rush of liquid rhyme, you utterly efface what is his distinguishing feature. No author probably is so difficult to translate such at least was Dr. Neale's opinion, and he had had experience enough of the difficulty to make him a judge; but, if translated at all, it can only be fairly done by adhering strictly to the lines upon which Adam himself builds his mellifluous superstructure. It is better, to my delight, to present even the skeleton of him, as one may hope to succeed in doing, in a perfectly literal translation; than to give him to the world as a shapeless mummy, embalmed though it may be in the richest pieces of original thought and feeling.

At the same time I would not be understood to maintain that no license at all is permitted to the translator; own versions of Adam of St. Victor would be more faulty, than I quite feel they are as it is, were that the case. I simply urge that the license must at any rate be limited, in the case of additions or omissions, to such as leave intact the sense of the original passages, and, in the case of meters, to, at most, the occasional varying the rhythm of some of them, leaving the number of syllables the same. Such a meter as the following, e.g., and there are some four or five of that character in Adam's collection of sequences, appears to me to be one, that it is almost impossible in our consonant ridden language to reproduce faithfully and yet gracefully.

Salve, dies dierum Gloria.

Dies felLx, Christi Victoria.

Dies digna jugi lastitia.

Dies prima!

I have ventured, therefore, to alter the emphasis, while keeping intact the length, of each line in this example;

> Hail, day, the glory of all days! to thee!
>
> Thrice happy day, Christ's day of victory!
>
> The first day, day most fit continually
>
> Our joy to show!

I have adopted the same course, and for the same reason, in the case of four other Sequences, viz.: "Gaude Sion, qu»diem recolis;" "Jerusalem et Sion filise;" "Aquas plenasamaritudine;" and "Gratiani gi ata solempnitas." A few lines, sprinkled about here and there in other Sequences, I have treated in the same way. With these exceptions, I have kept, I believe, rigidly to the exact meter of each original Sequence.

One great difficulty in carrying out the principle of literal translation in these volumes has been not only the number, but the character also, of the rhymes so called for. English rhymes are naturally, and generally, single rhymes; Latin rhymes, on the other hand, are naturally, and generally, double rhymes. In Latin, again, the same terminations, if attached to words of different meanings, are held to rhyme; in English, however, this is not the case, every word, in order to make a good rhyme, must in our language have a different termination, ultimate or penultimate, according as the rhyme is single or double, to the word with which it is meant to rhyme.

The literal translator, therefore, of any aspiring Latin poetry, especially one that ventures, in translating such a master of rhyme as Adam of St. Victor, to keep intact both the number and the character of the original rhymes, starts, handicapped, as it were, by the necessity of finding rhymes in numbers far greater than any English poetry, so far as I know, contains, and of a kind in which the English language is singularly poor. I venture to remind the critical reader of these facts, in the hope that they may serve to explain, if not to excuse, my shortcomings, which I am painfully aware of in the matter of rhymes. I can only say that I have done my best to avoid even doubtful rhymes, and such as still disfigure my translations remain, because I have failed to find better ones to replace them.

I have thought it better on the whole, chiefly in the interest of the translations, not to print the original sequences and my own renderings of them upon opposite pages. I am aware that some, who will value the book simply for the sake of the Latin text, would have preferred having the translations printed at the end of each volume by themselves, but the poetry of Adam of St. Victor is of so peculiar a kind, that I think the majority of any readers I may be fortunate enough to secure, will like better to not have the two placed as they arc for the sake of ready comparison. The translations, if found to be tolerably correct, are naturally such an interpretation of the originals as to render long critical notes unnecessary, and such as there are I have remitted to the end of each volume, so as not to interfere with the appearance of the pages.

The notes themselves are principally confined to short accounts of the less known Saints commemorated by the poet, to Scripture references, and to explanations of the typology and symbolism of both of which Adam is very fond contained in the Sequences. I have gathered my information from the best, indeed the only, sources accessible to me in a country parsonage. I should like to be able to thank by name all those who have aided me in many ways in my undertaking, but they are so many in number that I am compelled to content myself with a general expression of heartfelt gratitude in the case of the large majority of my kindly coadjutors. Some, however, I feel bound to mention more particularly.

A Historical Perspective of the "Victorines"

WHO ARE THE VICTORINES

ADAM of ST. VICTOR:

The Abbey of St. Victor, from which the great Latin hymnologist takes his name, and which, originally, was in the suburbs of Paris, was later on absorbed into the city itself, as she enlarged her borders, was celebrated, especially in the twelfth century, as a school of theology.

Probably no other religious foundation could boast of such a brilliant triad of doctors of divinity, as the one that graced this Abbey during that century in the persons of Hugh of St. Victor, known to his generation as the "Second Augustine;" his pupil, Richard of St. Victor, named Alter Augustine; and Adam of St. Victor, the author of the Sequences ' in these volumes, who, as will be apparent to the most cursory reader was even deeply versed in the learning of the school to which he belonged. If you were to place a "Greek" perspective, Hugh could be considered as Socrates, followed by his pupil Plato (Richard) and subsequently, Aristotle, (Andrew). The rational that I assert here is quite simple really; Hugh and Richard both followed an allegorical analysis of the scriptures, where as Andrew, like Chrysostom and Jerome, took a more straight forward approach. In the early days of the Christian church, there were two fundamental schools of thought: those who were form the "Antioch" side, and those of the "Alexandrian" segment. The Antioch's were literal, while the Alexandrian's were metaphorical. Thus, down through the ages and on into today's church, there remain these two formulary schools.

Beyond the fact, however, that they were monks of St. Victor, whose residence there one or other of them covered nearly the whole of the twelfth century, the accounts that we have left of them are exceedingly meager and uncertain; these being Andrew, a disciple under Richard and Archard. Andrew is considered as the "Second Jerome." Walter was also an abbot, but was an anti-intellectual, he wrote against Peter Abelard. They live for us now in days, very much as they must have lived, in the retirement of their monastic life, for their contemporaries, only in the books which they "Sequence." The prolongation of the versicle of the Alleluia, instituted in order to give the deacon time to reach the pulpit to chant the Gospel. Gradually words were set to this cadence, and so came the Sequence. It is ascribed alike to St. Notker and Alcuin; the Sequences in rhythm are a development of later days.

Originally the Sequence was called a Prose, because its early' form was rhythmical prose. Orby Shipley's "Glossary of Ecclesiastical Terms" (1872), wrote, of which, in all probability, we know more than their own generation did. Hugh of St. Victor, the oldest of them, was by birth a Saxon; when he entered the Monastery of St. Victor we are not told. All we can glean about his chronology is that he died there either in A.D. 1139, or one of the two following years.

Richard of St. Victor, his pupil, and a native of Scotland, was more closely contemporaneous with Adam, the last and most brilliant of the three. There seems no reason to doubt that he was nearly of the same age as the latter, though his life was by no means so prolonged as that of Adam, if we are to accept the authority of an old MS., quoted by Gautier, as quoted by John of Toulouse; which describes the poet as being "Richard Victoriana contemporaneous, sed longe superstes."

Regarding Adam of St. Victor so scanty are the materials for a biographical notice of him), we cannot certainly prove even the nationality. This much only seems to be certain, that he was a native either of England or Brittany. He is described generally in the MSS. of the period immediately succeeding his own as Brito, and the question remains, and must remain, unsettled, as to which of the two countries for which he is claimed as a native, that term refers. Of course in an Abbey where so many of the monks were evidently foreigners, for neither Hugh nor Richard were Frenchmen, it is possible that the great Medieval poet was a fellow countryman of ours; but Archbishop Trench and it is a point upon which, as upon most others, we may safely defer to his better judgment concludes, that "the fact that France was the main seat of Latin poetry in the twelfth century, and that all the most famous composers in this kind, as Hildebert, the two Bernards, Abelard, Marbod, Peter the Venerable, were Frenchmen, leaves it more likely that he, the first and fore most of all, was such as well!"

M. Gautier entertains no doubt, and he has evidently been most indefatigable in his researches into all that relates personally, or poetically, to the object of them, that, be he "Breton" or "Briton," Adam entered the religious foundation of St. Victor, as a young man, about A.D. 1130; after having, as Archbishop Trench says, "made his studies at Paris." Here he remained for the rest of his life, which was prolonged certainly to A.D. 11 72, and probably, according to M. Gautier, to A.D. 1192. And here he wrote at various times, as the occasion called each forth, the series, and it is not a short one, of the sequences on which his claim to literary honors mainly rests, and of which a great deal of English Churchmen must, in many points, decline to follow their doctrinal teaching very few will fail to recognize the exceeding beauty, looked at as classical compositions merely, and fewer still, one would hope, to appreciate at their real value the exactness of their author's theology when dealing with the great Catholic doctrines which are common to almost the whole of Christendom, or the devotional spirit that breathes throughout his writings.

Lord Coleridge, the present Lord Chief Justice of England, in his preface to a republication by him in 1872 of the seventeenth century edition in English of "A Mirror of Monks," by Lewis Blosius, (which we will produce later) expresses so completely the sentiments by which I have been animated in dealing with the works of Adam of St. Victor, that I gladly and gratefully avail myself of his lordship's permission to quote a few sentences from it here, feeling sure that the reader will be glad to have an opinion on such a point from one whose opinion upon any point must carry great weight with it

"It is hardly necessary to say that I do not agree with every theological doctrine which Blosius assumes or inculcates in his book; but I think the book in itself a good and beautiful book. I believe the writer of it to have been a holy man; and I do not think it right, in spite of high authority to the contrary, to mutilate or adapt such works as these. To do so appears to me unmanly and unfair. It is as if we were afraid of the soundness of our convictions, and dared not look in the face the fact that good men of other times did not share them. Whereas it is part of Christian history that very good and saintly men have held opinions in religion which we now think mistaken; and it is a narrow and shallow judgment which holds such opinions to be inconsistent with true and vital Christianity. This book, to my mind, proves that they are nowise inconsistent: and I most earnestly hope that those who read it carefully will think so too."

The reader will have the opportunity of judging for themselves as to the merits of the various sequences as they come before him; but it may be well, perhaps, to say a few words as to their general character, and I know not that they can be said better than by one who has so thoroughly identified his name with Latin hymnology generally, and especially with that of the "Victorine School," as the present Archbishop (Trench) of Dublin:

"Very different estimates have been formed of the merits of Adam of St. Victor's hymns. His most zealous admirers will hardly deny that he pushes too far, and plays overmuch with, his skill in the typical application of the Old Testament. So, too, they must own that sometimes he is unable to fuse his manifold learned allusion into the passion of his poetry. . . . Nor less must it be allowed that he is sometimes guilty of conceits, of plays upon words, not altogether worthy of the solemnity of his theme.

Thus of one Martyr he says,

' Sub securi stat securus; '

of another. Saint [Vincent] namely: —

' Dum torretur, non terretur;

of the Blessed Virgin (for he did not escape, as it was not to

be expected that he should, the exaggerations of his time),

' O dulcis vena venise; '

of heaven: —

' O quam beata curia,

Qus curse prorsus nescla.'

Sometimes, too, he is over fond of displaying feats of skill in versification, or prodigally accumulating, or curiously interlacing his rhymes, that he may show his perfect mastery of the forms which he is using, and how little he is confined or trammeled by them.

"These faults it will be seen, yet most are indeed of them but merits pushed into excess. Even accepting them as defects, his profound acquaintance with the whole circle of the theology of his time, and eminently with its exposition of Scripture; the abundant and admirable use, with indeed the drawback already mentioned, which he makes of it. Delivering as he does with his poems from the merely subjective cast of those, beautiful as they are, of St. Bernard, the exquisite are and variety with which for the most part his verse is managed and his rhymes disposed, their rich melody multiplying and ever deepening at the close. The strength which he often concentrates into a single line, his skill in conducting a story, and, most of all, the evident nearness of the things, which he celebrates to his own heart of hearts. All these, and other excellencies, render him, as far as my judgment goes, the foremost among the sacred Latin poets of the Middle Ages." (Tim, use for back cover)

"He may have no single poem to vie with the austere grandeur of the Dies Ircse, nor yet with the tearful passion of the Stabat Mater, although concerning the last point there might well be a question; but then it must not be forgotten that these stand well nigh alone in the names of ' Thus of a Roman governor, who, alternating flatteries with threats, is seeking to bribe St. Agnes from her allegiance to Christ by the offer of worldly dignities and honors,

"Offert multa, spondet plura,

Periturus peritura."

Their respective authors, while from his ample treasure house I shall enrich this volume with a multitude of hymns, all of them of considerable, some of the very highest, merit. Indeed, were I disposed to name any one who might dispute the palm of sacred Latin poetry with him, it would not be one of these, but rather Hildebert, Archbishop of Tours."

It would be unnecessary for me, even if I were able, which I am not, to add much to this eloquent and exhaustive summary of the merits, and defects as well, of this great poet. One point only, in what is characteristic of the author, is not touched upon, and that is his love of alliteration, carried at times perhaps to an excess like his play upon words,' but often used with striking effect.

The history of the Sequences in this work is a curious and a checkered one. As I said at the beginning of this notice, the Abbey of St. Victor, which in our poet's time was in the suburbs of Paris, was by the growth of the town afterwards included within its walls. There it remained undisturbed, and having Adam of St. Victor's poetry in its library, until the French Revolution, when, in common with all others, its religious foundation was dissolved, its inmates dispersed, and its precious MSS. removed, as it appeared afterwards, to the National Library in the Louvre. Some of Adam's Sequences had, during the centuries that the MSS. remained in the custody of the monks of the author's monastery, found their way into circulation, thirty-seven of them with his name attached to them, and a few others without any trace of them.

Take this instance from the Sequence, "On the Passion of St. Quintin,"

" Propter jugum Christi lene,

Premunt compes et catense

Carcerali clausum cella;

Sed triumphat bonus bene

Universum genus poense,

Famem, frigus, et flagella."

The thirty seven were collected and published by Ciichtoveus, a Roman Catholic theologian of the first half of the sixteenth century, in his "Elucidatorium Ecclesiasticum," which passed through several editions from 1515 to 1556 at Paris, Basle, and Geneva. This work, which was written originally for the instruction of the clergy in the meaning of the various offices of the Church, according to Archbishop Trench, became invaluable to those who made Mediaeval Hymnology their study, and was in fact the only collection of it on a large scale.

The remainder of the Sequences contained in these volumes, and which never saw the light (until they were discovered in the Louvre) from the date of the French Revolution up to the middle of this century, we owe to the persevering search after them which M. Gautier made about the latter date. Those published by him for the first time are forty-eight in number, and include some of the most striking of the whole collection. Of three the first line only survives, the remainder of the Sequences not having been found as yet; and it is more than probable that there may be more still written by Adam, which cannot be assigned to him now, because it is a remark able fact that, numerous as those hymns are of which he will henceforth have the credit, we do not possess a single Sequence of which he was professedly the author, upon so central a Christian truth as the Passion of our Lord, or one for Lent or Advent, which could hardly, one would imagine, have been the case always, seeing that the rest of the Christian year is so largely illustrated in his writings.

The collection, as M. Gautier gave it to the world, consisted of 106 "Sequences", satisfactorily proved to have come from Adam of St. Victor's pen, viz., thirty seven published and attributed to the author by Ciichtoveus, two published by him without attribution, seventeen published in other collections without attribution, forty seven published for the first time by Gautier, and the three mentioned above of which we have as yet only the first line. Besides these, however, there is the Epitaph of Adam, of which only the first ten lines were written by him, and eight Sequences doubtfully or wrongly attributed to him, but included in M. Gautier's volumes.

All these, arranged as they were in the French edition, will be found in that now offered to the public. The reader will, no doubt, be struck by the great variety of meters employed by the poet, not only in the Sequences, taken as a whole, but also in single Sequences. In some the meters changes several times during the course of them, and even single stanzas are constantly subjected to the same process. The effect is to give great variety to the hymns, generally and singly, enabling the poet to introduce an amount of light and shade into his compositions, which is impossible when one meter is rigidly adhered to throughout a poem. As all Adam's Sequences were originally set to music and used in the worship of his Abbey, a suggestion is perhaps allowable on my part, as to whether we might not now a days have some of the music in our choral services arranged upon a similar plan. As it is, we have nothing between the ordinary hymn in which the meter never changes, and for which, therefore, the same tune must be used throughout, and anthems, which, beautiful as they are, are far too elaborate and difficult for general use in our churches.

The arrangement of these Mediaeval hymns appears to me to combine the advantages, without the defects, of both hymns and anthems, possessing as they do all the simplicity of the first without their sameness, and much of the variety of the last without their elaborateness. If we could vary the tunes in a single hymn, as is often done, as it is, in the Te Deum or the Psalms of the day, we should be enabled to increase not only the length of the hymns, which are now confined to four or six verses, but to add to their devotional effect as well by having both the meter in which, and the music to which the words are set somewhat more appropriate to the sentiments sought to be expressed than is always the case now.

CONTENTS OF THE SECOND VOLUME

St. Vincent

The Conversion of St. Paul

The Purification of St, Mary the Virgin

The Annunciation of the Blessed Virgin Mary

The Annunciation of the Blessed Virgin Mary

The Invention of the Cross.

The Conversion of St. Augustine

St. Nereus and St. Achilleus

Reception of the Relics of St. Victor

The Nativity of St. John the Baptist

St. Peter and St. Paul

Commemoration of St. Paul

St. Margaret

St. Victor

St. Apollinaris

St. James the Greater

St. Germain

The Transfiguration of the Lord

St. Lawrence

The Assumption of the Blessed Virgin

St. Bartholomew

St. Augustine

The Beheading of St. John Baptist

St. Giles

The Nativity of the Blessed Virgin Mary

ST. VINCENT

See the longed-for day arriving!

Happy day, day pleasure giving!

Day in which we should delight!

Let us keep this day then holy,

On it Christ admiring truly,

As He does in Vincent fight.

For his birth, self-consecration,

Feeling, faith, speech, lofty station.

And his office eminent.

Under the paternal sway

Of Valerius his day

Of diaconate was spent.

Slow of speech, the bishop giveth

All his time to God, and leaveth

Preaching to the deacon's share:

Wreathed his words are with uprightness,

And his single mind with brightness. Bred of double learning, fair.

ST. VINCENT

When the truth that he believes

Sarragossa's crowd receives

From his lips through present grace,

Then the prefect's enmity,

Zealous for idolatry,

Fiercely would the church abase.

When their constant faith he learns, that never flagged,

To Valentia both in fetters to be dragged

He does direct.

Neither does the wretch that noble young man spare,

Neither to the holy bishop's age does care

To pay respect.

These men, tired with travel-pains,

Weighed down beneath a weight of chains,

In a foul jail he detains,

All food to them denies.

Though to hurt them he is fain,

Yet his wishes are in vain.

Since Christ's bounty does maintain

His own servants with supplies.

To exile by him is the old man sent.

The younger one meanwhile for punishment

The prefect keeps still graver.

What time his pain by claw and horse-rack ends,

Vincent at once the gridiron ascends

With spirit braced and braver.

As he burns, fears he spurns;

Even more to Christ he turns,

Nor, though present he discerns

The dread tyrant, for him cares:

Datian's cruel visage glows,

Tongue and hand each useless grows,

Till, such furious rage he shows,

He beside himself appears.

Into a cave then is the martyr thrown,

And, there confined, flung down on potsherds prone;

Still he enjoys much height unto him shown,

When angels bright to him appear.

At length, upon a pallet rudely cast.

He passes thence to heaven, his labors past;

And, thus triumphant, his brave soul at last

Is to his Prince presented there.

Datian no such grave alloweth,

As man's common law bestoweth:

Violence his malice doeth

To what law and nature say.

T. VINCENT

'Gainst the dead the fierce judge burns,

But more glory for him earns,

For the very wild beast turns,

Awe-struck, from its wonted prey.

Lo! untouched, a raven, flying,

Keeps the corpse, unburied lying,

And, a monstrous scheme thus trying,

Datian fails utterly.

But, unholy

Heathen's folly!

What earth would not,

What earth could not.

Waste, is hurried

To be buried

In the silent depths of sea.

Millstone's weight can hold him never,

Ocean must her dead deliver.

Whom the church would now endeavor

With one voice of praise for ever

To revere especially.

For his corpse, reduced to cinder,

Fire, earth, sea, illustrious render!

Jesus grant in mercy tender

We and all saints may Your splendor.

Duly praise at home with Thee! Amen.

ST. VINCENT

Tis a morn whence victory springs!

'Tis the glorious morn, that brings

Back this deacon's feast-day still:

Joy we all this morn so glorious,

Honoring, in Christ victorious,

Vincent the invincible.

He who bears this name of glory,

Viicent, proves the omen worthy

Of that name by what he dares:

Conquering, both by land and water,

Torturers' sharpest modes of slaughter,

Fearful pains and painful fears.

Like the curtain, which combines

Blue and scarlet tints, he shines

Round whose loins the girdle twines

Of a two-fold chastity.

T. VINCENT

Robes of fine twined linen wearing,

For the purple's palm preparing,

Tortures dire for Christ's sake bearing.

See him stand forth dauntlessly!

He, a victim fit for offering,

One of the red rams' skins covering

O'er the tabernacle's dome,

As he sows, true love's tears weeps,

In the sweat of his brow reaps,

But brings with him life's sheaf home.

Dragged to Datian's blood-stained dwelling

Datian there, devoid of feeling,

Sorely God's saint-servant tries.

First, the prefect does implore him,

Threatens now, now puts before him

This world's highest dignities.

Warrior-like, earth's glory spurning.

From the gifts, prayers, terrors, turning

Of despotic tyranny,

To a horse-rack is he fastened,

Where, while chastening, more is chastened

The despised chiefs vanity.

T. VINCENT

Red-hot bed o'er flames erected,

Lictor's stroke, or salt injected

Into inward parts laid bare,

Burn and torture all together.

Yet, with all their torments, neither

Drives this champion to despair.

Prison-bound, his limbs are riven

By sharp shards into them driven;

But a brightness, sent from heaven,

Soothes and heals him with its smiles:

There high honor his burden seems,

That dark cell with glory beams,

And as sweet as flowers he deems

Those sharp edges of the tiles.

When they to a soft couch move him.

He revives, and, as above him

Angels' tuneful notes approve him,

Yields his spirit to the Lord.

Thrown to wild beasts, help is shown him;

Ocean's billows cannot drown him;

But men with due honor crown him,

To his mother-earth restored.

Every element thus shines,

And with fitting signs combines.

In the victory this man winnes,

Fire and water, earth and air!

ST. VINCENT

Saint, best proof of truth supplying!

Pray you Christ, that, purifying

Us from sin, true joys undying

For the pure He will prepare,

That we may, with heaven's host vying,

In their alleluias share!

ST. VINCENT

Let the whole Church celebrate, —

Triumphs of a martyr great! —

Vincent's victories to-day!

To the King, who, whilst he fought,

Help, strength, armor, to him brought,

Praise and glory let us pay!

He, while still but young in years,

At the judgment-seat appears

Of the prefect Datian:

Word for word he gives again;

A grand controversy then,

Touching points of faith, began.

" There is nothing," Vincent saith,

" Truer than our holy faith:

" Christ I worship, Christ alone:

" Sire! the true God I declare,

" And reject those gods, which are

" No true gods, but wood and stone.

T. VINCENT

I despise your every threat,

And your mercy should regret

Therefore, torturer! rend and tear!

Then the prefect, big with wrath,

Fierce as wild beast in the path,

Cruel tortures does prepare.

He, upon the iron horse

Lifting him without remorse,

Racks him with long-lasting pain,

Till an iron heated frame.

Hissing with devouring flame,

Tears him from the rack again.

From its crossbars taken down,

Into prison is he thrown

On some potsherds' broken ends:

Whose sharp points to him appear

Sweetness with sweet flowers to share,

Till his soul to heaven ascends.

Forth to wild beasts is he cast;

They behold; they stand aghast;

By a bird is he watched o'er:

Sailors plunged him in the deep;

At his loss for joy they leap,

But his corpse now reaches shore.

 T. VINCENT

Thus, victorious every way,

Heaven and earth his power obey:

Let the Church rejoice and sing!

'Tis a day of victory,

'Tis a day of jubilee,

Which this feast to us does bring.

Martyr! in your blood, we pray.

Wash you all our sins away,

And primeval joys restore;

That, thus cleansed from sin's alloy,

We may in your glory joy

With all saints for evermore! Amen.

ONVERSION OF ST. PAUL

Let us joy, that Savior praising,

Hope in sinners' bosoms raising,

That they pardon will obtain.

When He Saul severely chided,

And, converted, called and guided

Back to Mother-Church again.

Saul, still threats and slaughter breathing,

With blood-thirsty purpose seething,

'Gainst the Lord's disciples tried,

Powers obtained for apprehending,

And, when bound, with torture rending

Those who served the Crucified.

As he journeyed, Jesus struck him

To the earth, and, to rebuke him,

With His radiance made him blind; 1

Till, once more his feet regaining.

He, a guiding hand obtaining.

In a lodging is confined.

 ONVERSION OF ST. PAUL

He laments, fasts, prays, believes,

Is baptized, his sight receives;

Changed to Paul that Saul became

Who had been our flock's oppressor;

Paul, henceforth our law's professor.

Into Paul thus changed his name.

Therefore, Paul, the Gentiles' teacher!

Chosen vessel! as our preacher,

Light on our dark hearts outpour;

And, for us your prayers employing,

Life for us obtain, destroying

Death that lasts evermore! Amen.

URIFICATION of MARY THE VIRGIN.

LET us, the heart's shrine preparing

With a heart renewed be sharing

In the old man's joy again,

Joy, which, held in his embraces,

So his long-felt heart's wish raises

Once more in the long-lived man.

Set an ensign for the nations,

Shrine with light, song with laudations,

Hearts with glory fills He;

Now a child for presentation,

When a man, a sin-oblation

On the Cross for sin to be!

Savior! here, here, Mary lowly!

Holy Son and mother holy!

Move us all to glad delight

By that work of light perfected,

Which we now, for prayer collected,

Image with our tapers bright!

URIFICATION *of MARY*

The true light the Word from heaven,

Virgin's flesh the wax, has given

To Christ's candle, bright as day,

Much to hearts that wisdom shows.

Through which virtue's path he knows.

Who by sin is led astray.

As one, love t'ward Jesus bearing,

In this festal custom sharing.

Doth a waxen taper hold,

So the Father's Word supernal,

Pledge of purity maternal.

Did old Simeon's arms enfold.

Joy you, who your Father barest!

Pure within, without the fairest!

From all spot or wrinkle free!

Pre-elect of the Beloved!

By the Elect of old approved!

Darling of the Deity!

Beauty of all kinds seems clouded,

Sore defaced and horror-shrouded.

When we see your beauty shine:

Bitter grows every savor,

Hateful and of filthy flavor,

After we have tasted thine.

 URIFICATION *of MARY*

Every scent the sweetest smelling

Seems not sweet, but most repelling,

With your scents our nostrils fill;

Love of all kinds is rejected

Instantly, or else neglected,

Whilst your love we cherish still.

Lovely light o'er ocean's waters!

Mother, peerless 'mongst earth's daughters!

Parent true of truth immortal!

Way of life to grace's portal!

Medicine all the world to heal!

Duct of wine from life's fount bursting.

For which all men should be thirsting!

Sweet to those in health or sickness!

Health to all, who in sore weakness

For its cheering draught appeal I

Fountain duly

Sealed as holy!

Outpour for us

Rivers o'er us:

Fount of showers

For hearts' flowers!

Water ever

From your river

To all thirsting souls impart:

Fount o'erflowing!

Through hearts going,

URIFICATION of MARY

Grant ablution

From pollution:

Fountain, given

Pure from heaven!

From earth, wholly

Impure, throughly

Purify man's impure heart! Amen.

NNUNCIATION OF THE BLESSED VIRGIN MARY

GABRIEL, sent from heaven to carry,

As Christ's faithful emissary,

Greetings to the Blessed Mary,

Sacred words with her rehearsed:

Good and sweet the word he takes

As he in her chamber speaks.

And of " Eva" " Ave " makes,

Having Eve's name thus reversed.

Comfort gives he, fear dispelling,

" By the Holy Ghost's in-dwelling,

" You the Highest's shadow veiling,

" You," says he, " shall bear the Lord! "

— "Be it so," by her was spoken,

" To His handmaid by this token;

" Let my virgin seal unbroken

" Be, according to your word! "

As that promise thus declares,

The incarnate Word appears:

But the virgin ever shares

Still intact virginity.

 # ANNUNCIATION OF THE BLESSED VIRGIN MARY

Such a birth no mother shows;

She, whom mortal man ne'er knows,

Pain nor labor undergoes,

When she bears her progeny.

Of a wonder new you hearest:

Have but faith, 'twill then be clearest:

This shoe's latchet, if you nearest,

You are powerless to untie.

Great the lesson is, none higher!

In the bush and in the fire;

With feet shod let none draw nigher.

Lest he come unworthily.

The dry rod, without a shower,

In new manner, through new power,

Fruit produced as well as flower:

So a maid has borne a son!

Blessed be that fruit for ever,

Fruit of joy, of sorrow never!

Had he tasted its sweet savor,

Adam ne'er had been undone.

Jesus, gentle as none other.

Holy son of holy mother,

King of heaven, is, as our brother,

To a manger-cradle brought.

NNUNCIATION OF THE BLESSED VIRGIN MARY

May He, thus for our salvation

Born, effect our guilt's purgation,

Seeing that our occupation

Of this earth with risk is fraught. Amen.

 # ANNUNCIATION OF THE BLESSED VIRGIN MARY

HE bridesman thus salutes a maid on earth,

And tells the order of a wondrous birth:

" Lo! " says he, " you, blessed one!

" Shall conceive and bear a son,

" Nor shall know your virgin zone

" Has been broken! "

Forewarned by the grace of God

Now, but doubtful of the mode,

She, since naught she understood,

Asks a token.

Fear you not, Oh blessed Mary!

Show your faith, for faith can carry

You through this effectually.

Care and doubt, Oh Mary! still your,

Since a mother by God's will your,

With no man allied, shall be.

NNUNCIATION OF THE BLESSED VIRGIN MARY

In a virgin's womb, her Son,

Thus the Word incarnate lay;

But the nature of the one

Took the other's not away.

Oh thing most strange and blest!

Love most wonderful indeed!

The Godhead, close compressed,

Lies in a manger-bed!

Oh Child exceeding wise!

Oh Word that whines and cries!

Oh majestic lowliness!

Both help us and direct.

And, as the Word, protect,

Like us in our fleshly dress!

Mary, who thus God conceivest.

And the sinner's hopes revivest!

After God to hope you givest

Strength and confidence well-tried.

Jesus, mighty and endearing!

Jesus! at our head appearing,

Grant we may Your lot be sharing

By Your side.

Through Your mother glorified! Amen.

NVENTION OF THE CROSS

To the Cross its due laudation

Let us give; our exultation

Is its special glory bright:

'Tis the Cross our victory sends,

Victory sure, that never ends,

O'er our fierce foe in the fight.

Sweet strains! flow you,

Heavenward go you!

Since for sweetest

Strains the meetest

Count we you, sweet tree! to be:

But let life and voice be one,

For with these in unison,

Dulcet is the symphony.

Let its servants' praise be given

To the Cross, which life in Heaven,

Joyous gift! for them prepares:

NVENTION OF THE CROSS

Yea, one and all, let them its praise rehearse:

All hail! Salvation of the universe!

Tree, that man's salvation bears!

Oh the blissful exaltation

Of this altar of salvation,

Reddened with the Lamb's blood spilt!

E'en the Lamb without a stain.

Who has cleansed the world again

From the first man's sin and guilt!

Ladder this to sinners given,

By which Christ, the King of heaven,

All things to Himself has led;

Whose form, rightly comprehended,

Shows that its four arms, extended

Wide, o'er earth's four quarters spread.

No new mystery we mention;

'Tis not recent the invention

Of this doctrine of the Cross:

Marah's waters did it sweeten;

And the flint, by Moses beaten

With it, did its torrents toss.

For a house no guard avails,

O'er whose lintel a man fails

To erect the Cross's sign:

NVENTION OF THE CROSS

Sword ne'er smote, nor son was lost,

In the dwelling, whose door-post

Bore aloft the mark divine.

In Sarepta, two sticks gleaning,

The poor v,'idow of attaining

Sure relief good hope did feel;

And, without faith's sticks we use,

Nought avails the oil's small cruse,

Nor the little store of meal.

In the Scriptures,

'Neath type-pictures,

Lie these latent,

But now patent,

Benefits the Cross bestows;

Faith kings cherish;

Foemen perish;

One crusader,

Christ his leader,

Puts to flight a thousand foes.

Rome beheld those vessels founder,

Bridging o'er the river round her.

And Maxentius with them drown:

Thracians flying, Persians dying.

Prone too was the foes' chief lying,

By Heraclius o'erthrown.

NVENTION OF THE CROSS

'Tis the Cross their courage wakes,

And its own victorious makes;

Hence disease and weakness takes;

Doth the powers of hell restrain;

Freedom to the captive givesth,

And new life to all that liveth;

Yea, in everything reviveth

Their old glory once again.

Cross! farewell, you tree of glory!

This world's true salvation's story!

Not a tree is there before thee

Ranked for leaf or bud or flower:

Christian medicine! health assure your

To the whole; the sick man cure your:

In your name, so high and pure, now

Things are done which pass man's power.

You, from whom the Cross draws blessing!

Hear us now Your praise confessing,

And, when this life here is ended,

Those, who on it have attended,

In the halls of true light place.

Serving You, should torments try us.

Grant those torments may pass by us:

When the day of wrath draws nigh us,

With eternal joys supply us

Richly of Your bounteous grace! Amen.

ONVERSION OF ST. AUGUSTINE

LET all the faithful tell around

Augustine's praises publicly;

And tongue, heart, life, together sound

In spiritual ecstasy!

Our father's solemn festal rites,

Returning to us year by year,

Invite us to those pure delights,

Which nevermore shall disappear.

Well-learned in all those arts was he,

Which "liberal " we account to be;

And in all Scriptures equally,

From which his thoughts were never free.

At first, puffed up with earthly lore,

Which neither end nor object knew.

He wished unseen things to explore

By light his senses on them threw.

ONVERSION OF ST. AUGUSTINE

Whilst he was still a Gentile youth,

He falls into that error's snares,

Which would believe as very truth,

That fig-trees, stripped of leaves, shed tears.

When there from Carthage he had come

To lecture upon rhetoric,

You called him, Oh Lord! at Rome

To the true faith, the Catholic.

When, by God's will and not his own,

He comes to Milan to reside,

To Ambrose there becoming known,

He straightway takes him for his guide.

When afterwards he was baptized

By that blest prelate, through he

The pomp of this poor world despised,

And changed his life most wondrously.

He, whilst his studies he directs

Towards the words of Holy Writ,

The witness for all time collects

Of many a writer touching it.

He 'gainst the Manichaean sect

Proved an insuperable wall; *

And by his preaching a respect

Most wonderful obtained from all.

ONVERSION OF ST. AUGUSTINE

When Monica his mother, who

Had come from Africa, first knew

Of the conversion of her boy,

Her heart within her leaped for joy.

For she beholds that very son,

Once as a Manichsean known,

Converted from his former state,

Seeking his Lord to imitate.

Illustrious pastor! us, we pray,

Who now thine endless praise declare,

From this world's ruin and decay

Preserve you by unceasing prayer.

Jesus! sweet refuge, where those slake

Their griefs, who refuge with You take!

Grant us for this our father's sake

A good departure hence to make. Amen.

TS. NEREUS & ACHILLEUS

The triumph let us celebrate

Of Nereus and Achilleus now,

Whom faith's bright ardor did translate

To endless glory from below.

Grooms of the bedchamber they both

To virgin Domitilla were,

True servants of the God of truth,

Mirrors of purity most rare.

By Peter's ministry were they

To the pure font of baptism brought,

And to the maiden they display

The precious truths that Christ had taught.

Led by the arguments they use

Of spot or wrinkle to be ware,

With her whole soul does she refuse

The couch of mortal spouse to share.

TS. NEREUS & ACHILLEUS

By Clement's sacred hands arrayed

In sacred robes, within is stirred

With fire of holy zeal this maid,

Whene'er the name of Christ is heard.

Therefore Aurelian's vengeful wrath

'Gainst Domitilla breaks forth,

And her he would before have wed

He plans to punish now instead.

As, roused by anger's sting, he raves,

Christ's handmaid off by him is sent,

Together with these two, her slaves.

To Pontia's isle in banishment.

Prisons and Furius, who were there.

In Simon Magus' footsteps trod;

Perverting with too zealous care

The simple from sound faith in God.

Then Nereus and Achilleus both

With arguments gainsay their lies;

And at the preaching of the truth

The pervert from his error flies.

With torture, to the horse-rack borne.

Is Nereus with Achilleus torn;

But not a whit the lictor stirs

Christ's to be idol-worshippers.

TS. NEREUS & ACHILLEUS

Flames with their mangled limbs are fed,

And they, beheaded here, again

Are re-united with their Head,

Who does in heavenly places reign.

Grant through their merits, and their prayer

In efficacy unsurpassed,

Of that one Head's one body there

We members be, though least and last.

May Domitilla Flavia be

Our help to a like constancy,

Who, like to men in victory,

Can boast their glory equally! Amen.

ECEPTION *of the RELICS of ST. VICTOR*

From the root of true afection,

And from pious predilection,

Let this church's anthem rise!

Let both heart and Lips be singing,

And let all from Victor springing

Joy in Victor's victories.

His remains, now to us granted,

From Marseilles have been transplanted

Hither by a faithful few;

So that whom before in spirit

We possessed, we now inherit

In corporeal presence too,

'Tis our joy's full consummation;

Let us show our exultation

From the bottom of the heart.

ELICS of ST. VICTOR

For this martyr's relics raise

Matter for unceasing praise,

And an endless joy impart.

May the organ of our soul,

And our flesh's drum, control

Every strain of melody,

With themselves in discord found.

And take part in all whose sound

Is with theirs in harmony!

As with choirs in unison,

Of our habits too but one

Should the modulation be:

Voices in a different key,

Habits that no law obey,

Gravely hinder harmony.

Sounds by different lips outpoured

Must discordant strains afford,

If the finger of the Lord

First attune not every chord

With a gentle mastery.

If the Spirit's sweetening power

Touch the heart not to the core,

Then the voice's loudest roar,

And earth's joys in richest store,

Will be tasteless inwardly.

ECEPTION of the RELICS of ST. VICTOR

Men, with minds distracted, never

Feel the sweetness thence distilled;

Neither are life's true charms ever

Unto us on earth revealed.

May believers here unite

But to taste of joys so bright,

Taste, and thirst for their delight,

Till they there shall be full filled!

Let our hearts' mouth taste its flavor,

That through its internal savor

We may show no further favor

To this world's seductive love:

'Tis a savor salutary,

'Tis a taste extraordinary,

Which does in oblivion bury

Earthly cares 'mongst which we move.

That the world to us be bitter.

May Christ's perfume seem still sweeter,

And this sweetness ever greater

Grow within our inmost hearts:

Where such fragrance round us flows,

Spiritual fervor grows,

And for all, that earth bestows

Passingly, the love departs.

ELICS *of ST. VICTOR*

Victor, soldier now victorious!

Of Christ's martyrs the most glorious!

From sins here to souls injurious

Keep us, lest a love all-spurious

Sink us in iniquity:

With one heart and voice before thee,

Giving you especial glory,

Strive we honor to assure thee!

Show us favor, we implore thee,

Whilst we travel o'er this sea!

Ne'er permit their hope's frustration,

Who are your own congregation;

Cause to Christ our presentation.

That we may by contemplation

Now with you His glory know.

Christ! to You due honor paying,

Have the words we have been saying

Been Your champion's praise portraying;

Whilst he here with us is staying,

Let no griefs our joys o'erthrow! Amen.

ATIVITY of ST. JOHN the BAPTIST

LET the Church now in Your honor

Celebrate once more the feast

Of the Baptist, Your forerunner,

On his natal day, Oh Christ!

Thus we praise the King's own power

In His very herald's cry,

Whom He does with virtues dower,

And by office magnify.

Gabriel a promise making

To the elder of a son;

When he doubted, power of speaking

Lost the unbelieving one.

Born the child is, the declarer,

Standard-bearer,

Trump, of law and monarch new.

*ATIVITY of ST. JOHN the BAPTIST*

A voice the Word precedes,

The bridegroom's man the bridegroom leads,

Star of morn, the sunrise too.

She by speaking,

He, signs making,

Both his parents name their son:

At which token

Fetters, broken.

Off his sire's dumb tongue were thrown.

John's birth was prognosticated

By a word from heaven come, '

And beforehand demonstrated,

While he yet was in the womb.

That o'er-ripened age conceiveth,

A suggestive lesson giveth;

Dark truths declares

That long-barren womb that bears!

'Gainst the laws of nature truly

Was this John's conception wholly:

Such a birth must be

Grace's work, not nature's, solely.

In her womb a virgin-mother

Prisons God, which babe this other

From the womb's straits does applaud.

ATIVITY of ST. JOHN the BAPTIST

Openly the voice, that cries

In the waste, the Lamb descries,

Voice, the herald of the Word!

Bright his faith and clear his speech is,

And he many a thousand teaches.

And does to the true light bring.

He its lantern, not that light, is;

Christ that light for ever bright is,

Light that lights everything.

Camels' hair his clothing made he,

Girded with a leathern zone;

Locusts and wild honey had he

To support his life alone.

There has not arisen any

Greater, — on Christ's testimony, —

Of a woman born than he:

Christ the one exception makes,

In that flesh of flesh he takes

Without fleshly agency.

Martyr holy!

Through we truly

Guilty are; to honor thee

All-unworthy;

ATIVITY of ST. JOHN the BAPTIST

As your praises

Fond hope raises,

Hear us of your clemency,

We implore thee!

Now on this your birthday give us

Gladness promised thence to come;

Nor of like delight deprive us

In your laurelled martyrdom.

While such mystery

In your history,

Lost in wonder, we revere.

May Christ through thee

Now renew the

Comfort of His presence here! Amen.

STS. PETER & PAUL

ROME! St. Peter celebrate you!

Rome! St. Paul too venerate you

With an equal reverence!

Let the church be joyful truly,

And, rejoicing in them wholly,

Praise them with a joy intense!

These, on whom the Church is grounded,

Founded by them, on them founded,

Are her bases and roof-props;

Curtains and the tent above her

Those red skins that form her cover;

And her flowers, bowls and knops.

Clouds they are, light radiating.

Human heart-soil irrigating.

Now with dew and now with rain: 1

Preachers for a new law pleading,

Leaders to Christ's safe fold leading

A new flock of Christian men.

TS. PETER & PAUL

Together toiling, they

Thresh out the barn-stored grain,

In hope that thus they may

The vineyard's penny gain.

And, as they wield the fan.

Away the chaff is blown,

While 'neath fresh fruits again

The crowded barn-floors groan.

" Mountains " is their appellation.

Catching first illumination

From the light of the true Sun.

Such their virtue is, that even

Names like " firmament " and " heaven "

Have by it for them been won.

They the rout of sickness cause.

And, repealing grim death's laws,

Evil spirits put to flight:

They destroy idolatry,

And from guilt the guilty free,

Making sad hearts once more bright.

Both a common glory share in,

Each of them however bearing

Marks of greatness all his own:

TS. PETER & PAUL

Peter, peerless prince, presides

O'er the whole church; Paul provides

Laws to govern it well-known.

But to one is princedom given,

That the true faith, never riven

By disputes, be one as well:

Many seeds does one shell cover,

But the strength is one moreover

Of the many 'neath that shell.

Coming to Rome, they met

Salvation to proclaim,

For they well knew that it

Was full of deeds of shame,

Yet no cure discerning.

'Gainst those iniquities

These true physicians fight,

Whose saving remedies

Those fools oppose with might,

Never wisdom learning.

As Christ's truth they there expounded.

Nero, by their words confounded,

Simon Magus too, astounded.

Yield not to the apostles' word.

STS. PETER & PAUL

Weakness flies, death's self dies,

Rome believeth, Magus sighs;

New life earth revives,

Now its idols are abhorred.

Wicked Nero, captivated

With the doctrines Magus stated,

By his death now desolated,

Mourns his dreadful headlong fall;

But these warriors pre-elected,

Ne'er from faith's straight line deflected.

In the battle undejected

Stand, whom sword can ne'er appal.

Peter, who true light enjoys,

On the cross, head downward, dies;

Paul by swordsman's stroke; whose passion.

Though thus differing in its fashion,

A reward, not differing, gains.

Fathers, highest rank attaining!

With the King of all kings reigning!

May the judgment, so sustaining.

Of your power for us be gaining

A release from sinful chains! Amen.

STS. PETER & PAUL

ROME! rejoice, earth's mistress reckoned!

In the victory of the second

Praised should the first pastor be.

Joy let all the world be showing,

And its zeal for virtue growing

Greater in his memory.

Holy love's bright torch is Peter,

Truth's light, salt that makes sweeter,

Mount that righteousness displays,

Well that from the Savior wells,

Fruitful tree that sweetly smells,

Tree that no decay decays.

How aright tell Peter's story?

Though unseen Christ's works of glory.

At the first suggestion made

Nets and ship at once he leaves,

Ere the full truth he receives

Through the quickening Spirit's aid.

TS. PETER & PAUL

Gold nor silver coin possessing,

Bright with miracles is he,

Who, the lame man's nerves releasing,

Bursts their fetters instantly.

From his palsy liberated,

Once once more upright stands,

When, by Peter supplicated,

God unto his prayer attends.

Life to Dorcas Peter giveth.

And a youth from death reviveth,

With a power from limit free:

On the stormy waves he treadeth,

Whom the Savior's right hand leadeth,

When he follows falteringly.

When his faith Christ's question tries

In his answer he supplies

Briefly what must be our creed:

Christ the Son of God avowing,

But the fitting difference showing

In Him as the woman's seed.

His denial, thrice repeated,

Love, love only, expiated,

And confession three times made.

'Tis an angel lets loose

Peter from the prison-house.

Where he, doomed to die, was laid.

STS. PETER & PAUL

Weakness 'neath his shadow ceases,

Mind and body's heath increases;

Impotent become diseases

Through this great physician's power.

Magus hate for Peter feels,

Peter Magus' craft reveals,

And men's hearts by preaching steels

'Gainst his subtle magic lore.

From a rock his name deriving,

Peter, in fierce conflict striving,

Conquers, though, whilst he is living,

Lasts the contest's struggle dire.

Magus, as aloft he flies,

Falls headlong down and dies,

And, most justly stricken, lies

'Neath the judgment of God's ire.

Nero fumes infuriated,

Nero for this monster mourns,

Nero, 'gainst whose empire hated

All the world complaining turns.

So he Peter's cross prepares

Through his crimes' abettors then,

Whereon Christ is, Christ declares,

Crucified in him again.

TS. PETER & PAUL

To Peter's care Christ's sheep are given,

Who holds as well the keys of heaven:

From Peter goes that sentence forth,

Which binds and looses all on earth.

Oh for our shepherd's merits' sake,

And prayers that our salvation win,

From us. Eternal Shepherd! take

Our debt to You for all our sin! Amen.

TS. PETER & PAUL

This triumphal day returning

Is a type of endless morning,

Counterpart of glory bright:

'Tis a happy, glad, day truly,

When for victory great and holy

Peter arms him for the fight

Simple, poor, unknown, he seeketh,

From what he in fishing taketh,

His sole means of livelihood:

To him are the keys of heaven —

A poor man but faithful — given.

And to find Christ's flock their food.

Through the sea his nets he hauls,

But, when from the sea Christ calls.

Thence he at His call is led;

Quits his oar, his draw-net spurning,

Leaves his vessel, Christ discerning,

By His word thenceforth is fed.

TS. PETER & PAUL

He has given to him another

Oar, a net unlike his other,

And a different vessel now:

For his oar the key of heaven,

For his net God's word, is given,

For his ship God's Church below.

'Gainst him, like the waves of ocean,

This world's flood of deep emotion.

Fears and sorrows fiercely beat;

Which gives wolves a lamb-like nature,

And, as offerings, every creature

Brings to God, both great and small.

Of God's flock is he the pastor,

Steward of an heavenly master.

And a fisherman of men:

Walking on the sea he goes,

Sinking fast, when fear he shows,

On the Lord he calls then.

A new name he now possesses,

Peter! rock! when he confesses

Christ the Son of God to be.

Sound that faith is, true that teaching,

Not from flesh, — from heaven's self reaching!

Emanates this mystery.

# STS. PETER & PAUL

Unto Peter are committed

Two keys; one for scales is fitted,

Wherein merits' weight to weigh:

One the key of power is, binding

Freedom's fount, or paths ascending

Opening to the reahns of day.

Peter, having thrice denied Him

Whom he loved, wept, when beside Him

He looked round who heals grief:

Cleansing is that balmy river

Of sad tears sore hearts deliver,

And that sigh, fond heart's relief

Why, Oh man! are you so haughty?

Think'st to stand amidst this naughty

World's calamities and cares?

Ne'er presume you; Peter sins:

Ne'er despair; since Peter wins

Pardon for his guilt by tears!

With his wretched wife the lying

Ananias is found dying,

A most righteous fate is such!

Life the word of life, see! giveth!

Tabitha at once reviveth,

When she feels St. Peter's touch.

STS. PETER & PAUL

Close confined by Herod's orders

In the prison's penal borders,

Fetters stiffening every limb;

Soft the iron's hardness grows,

Doors fly open, no man knows;

'Tis an angel sent to him!

Rome, earth's head, sin's source, chief center

Where the plague of crime dare venture,

Rome, that Rome, does Peter enter,

By the Spirit's sword on borne;

Since death's chieftain he o'erthrows,

Life's light to the blind he shows,

Treating, while Paul with him goes,

Nero's dreadful cross with scorn.

Simon, mad, an height ascended

And fell headlong; Paul's life ended

'Neath the sword; and, limbs extended,

Nailed is Peter to the tree:

Thus both taught and teacher, whether

Lover or beloved either,

Savior thus and saved together,

Share the cross's agony.

Peter! from your net selected,

Draw us where, with joy perfected,

Sion is on high erected.

And the true Lamb's feast is spread;

STS. PETER & PAUL

Where is rest from this Hfe's fever,

Where night follows daylight never,

Where in endless Hfe for ever

Man shall like to God be made! Amen.

OMMEMORATION of ST. PAUL

Knock with heart and voice at heaven,

Gentile Church! for victory given

Loud triumphant paeans sing!

Paul, the Gentiles' teacher, now,

Life's course finished here below,

Is in glory triumphing!

He, a Benjamin, when younger,

With a fierce wolf's ravening hunger,

Hostile to believers is.

At morn a wolf, at eventide a sheep,

He, when a star illumes his darkness deep.

Teaches Gospel verities.

He to the way of death holds fast,

Till life's way seizes him at last.

As he to Damascus speeds;

Threats he breathes, now faith avoweth;

Prostrate now, obedience showeth;

Whom now bound another leads.

 OMMEMORATION of ST. PAUL

To Ananias is he sent;

Thus to the sheep the fierce wolf went;

Cruel zeal no longer burns.

Fontal rite he undergoes;

Water, whence salvation flows,

Poison into spiced wine turns.

Sacred vessel, blest of heaven,

Vessel, whence the sweets are given

Of doctrinal grace's wine,

He the synagogue goes round.

And the faith of Christ does found

On the prophets' previous line.

He the Cross's word declares,

Sufferings for its sake he shares,

Thousand different deaths he dies:

But still a living victim he

Abides through unquelled constancy,

Victor o'er all agonies!

Set apart, to Gentiles preaching,

He the wise of this world's teaching

Foils through wisdom from on high.

Caught up to the third heaven, his eyes

The Father and the Son likewise

In one substance there descry.

 **COMMEMORATION of ST. PAUL**

Mighty Rome and learned Greece in turn

Bow their necks and wondrous mysteries learn:

Spreads the faith of Christ abroad.

Christ's Cross triumphs; Nero fums;

And, since faith fast waxed, he dooms

Paul its preacher to the sword.

From him thus his flesh-load casting,

Paul the true Sun everlasting

Sees, the Father's only Son:

In light he looks upon the light;

Oh may we through his influence bright

Never have in hell to groan. Amen.

ST. MARGARET

WHILST now Sion's trump rejoices,

Let the clergy's measured voices

In the church sing joyfully!

For to-day a spouse of heaven

To her rest on high is given

With supreme felicity.

Margaret, a virgin martyr,

In glad triumph her departure

Takes to heaven's heights far away:

Thus for ever there she shareth

Lo, its rewards, since here she feareth

Not the tortures of a day.

She, a simple shepherdess,

As a sheep before the face

Of a wicked wolf, is made

Prey for cruel butchers' blade.

 T. MARGARET

But no tortures break her down,

Nor by soft words is she won;

For she weighs the wage she gains,

In preferring penal pains.

She, when in her prison sleeping,

Ever careful watch there keeping,

Prays that no seducer creep in

Through those butchers' cunning fraud.

To the Bridegroom, bowed, she prayeth,

Boldly spurns what Satan sayeth,

And in each case thus obeyeth

The commandment of the Lord.

From prison brought,

Is she stretched out,

Whilst upon a rack they tie her:

Beat black and blue,

Nigh burnt up too.

Is she with scourge and flames of fire.

The blood does from her gush

And cover o'er the flesh

Wholly of this virgin:

Though of such impious fame,

Olybrius feels shame.

Whilst the foul crime urging.

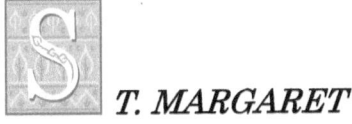 T. MARGARET

Into water plunged, she smarts,

As the chill that it imparts

Doth to burnings' heat succeeded

But, therein regenerated,

She the dove's wage contemplated

In the heavens above her head.

Lo! a dragon, as she lay

In her prison's inmost bay.

Doth the maid devour;

But the Cross of high renown,

Signed ere she was swallowed down,

Frees her from its power.

To the devil, as she pressed him

Underneath her virgin feet,

Spoke this dove, ere she released him,

When he sought her from the pit.

Time she gained for prayer, then offered

To the sword her head and suffered,

Living victim of the Lord!

O'er the world she triumphed, dying,

And, the second death defying,

To the heavenly mansions soared.

ST. MARGARET

This bright day let gratulations,

Virgin! by earth's joyful nations

Evermore to Christ be poured!

Sing, ye glad crowd now before us!

" Virgin Margaret, hail! " in chorus,

" Martyr worthy of the Lord! "

With the heavenly company,

In the sight of light most high,

You enjoy endlessly

Comfort for your pain and woe:

Of the Bridegroom ask, that He

With the price He deigned to be,

As our Savior, us would free

From destruction by the foe! Amen.

T. VICTOR

HOLY band! behold, a morning

Of full triumph is returning;

With a holy joy rejoice;

Heartfelt be your adoration,

And your inward exultation

Publish with uplifted voice.

Joyful can the heart be never,

Till itself from earth it sever,

Made from its contagion free:

Would'st you live? This world then fleeing,

Test the love of this world's being

Hushed to sleep within you be.

Victor in his youth's first flower,

Rather Christ's in-dwelling power

By His grace, the victory won:

O'er the world and flesh victorious,

Vanquished he man's foe all-furious,

Victor but by faith alone!

T. VICTOR

Martyr invincible! Your wondrous victory

Wondrously moves us to wondrous felicity;

Mother-church! bringing forth songs of glad jubilee,

Praise in His soldier your King's mighty deeds for thee!

Christ's brave soldier, never tired,

Scorns with wages to be hired.

As a Christian, for the strife:

He but to a crown aspires,

Nor the usual pay desires

To support his mortal life.

The chief Asterius

With his most impious

Comrade Eutitius,

Equally barbarous,

Treat him most cruelly:

Dragged first the streets along,

He to a rack is strung,

Then tortured as he hung;

Unbroken still by wrong

His martyr-constancy.

Bright and tearless,

Of life careless,

Stands the fearless

Champion, peerless

Victor o'er pains untold!

ST. VICTOR

In his anguish

Never languish

His mind's powers,

Neither cowers

His stout heart so brave and bold.

For that stand, his foot they sever,

But yet still the maimed stump never

From the path that Christ trod strayed:

Glad for Christ his foot he loses,

Who for Christ his head too chooses

Shall an offering soon be made.

Joy to lose his foot he showeth,

Ne'er his faith 'neath torture boweth;

E'en as mustard stronger groweth,

As the more its grains we bruise.

Fierce the torturer's fury burns

'Gainst him, but to stupor turns,

When he Victor's strength discerns.

Which Christ's presence there renews.

First beneath a mill-stone shivered.

And his head then from him severed,

He from life was so delivered,

As, when death its worst endeavored,

An immortal prize to gain.

T. VICTOR

In your Victor's high laudation

Joy, Oh holy congregation!

Heart, hand, voice, with acclamation

Close this great day's jubilation

With a loud triumphant strain! Amen.

T. VICTOR

In Easter-Tide.

Preface. Let all Christians sound the praise of the

blessed martyr Victor!

MAXIMIAN the cruel has— inflicted death

upon him, — and thus blessings, will he,

nill he, won him.

Life and death together fought

in a strife with wonder fraught:

Christ's own martyr slain

lives to reign.

." Say, in your agony

what, Oh champion!

didst you see? "

"I saw the banner of Christ reigning,

— His glory too, who soothes complaining."

Tortures' sore distresses

with signs are his witnesses: at whose petitions dead bodies

come to life, and — healed are infirmities.

ST. VICTOR

. Far rather should we believe Christ's Church alone

than a race perverse, who have evil done.

Thus we know that you do reign now;

Place for us to gain now by you,

great Victor, deign you! Amen,

ST. JAMES the GREATER

LET our choir in sweet laudation,

Sounding with clear intonation,

Chant a new-made song to-day:

'Tis with James the lyre resounds,

Who with merits rare abounds

In so wonderful a way.

He and Zebedee his father

Toiled as fisheniien together

By the Sea of Galilee:

Jewry's withered fig-tree bore him,

And, as his stern nurse, watched o'er him

In the Law's severity.

Hearing a voice divine God's will proclaim.

He, when Christ's nod and look commands the same,

Abjures at once the fisher's trade and name,

Scenting afar eternal gifts outpoured:

 *T. JAMES the GREATER*

He gives the Church the Synagogue's old place,

Changes his sire for God, the law for grace,

Transforming of set purpose in each case

Ship to the cross and nets to God's own Word.

He, pure vessel! grain most feeding!

Drinks milk from God's word proceeding.

Sucks the breasts of life on high,

The Apostolate assumeth,

A great prince in Heaven becometh,

With the word attacks the sky.

The great King of glory he

Doth in all his beauty see.

With his visage bright as flame,

Who, when now the cross drew nigh,

Was in his fierce agony

Sprinkled with a blood-sweat stream.

Him too at that mystic feast

With the Lamb's divine flesh Christ

Fed most truly;

And his soul with heavenly fire

Did the Paraclete inspire

Fully, throughly.

He, his twain wings exercising.

Sets a ladder, heavenward rising,

Of words said and actions done;

 T. JAMES the GREATER

And of Magians, God opposing,

Wildest thoughts and doctrines choosing,

Makes the faith with angels' one.

By this Hebrew's voice were given

Wakening sounds Uke God's in heaven,

Teaching a lost world that even

Its sins penitence could heal:

James like vivid lightning glows,

Bright width marks that virtue shows,

Thought on things divine bestows,

And for heaven expends his zeal.

Herod therefore, hot with passion,

Wild with direst indignation,

Forth his cruel mandate sent,

Ordering him to death most dreaded,

With the sword to be beheaded.

Who deserved no punishment.

Thus, martyrdom's fierce frost all thawed and past,

St. James's wisdom wins for him at last

The crown which is the victor's prize.

Through whose assistance now the Church does shine:

May its faith stand, its grace too ne'er decline.

But gain at last its guerdon in the skies! Amen.

RANSFIGURATION OF OUR LORD.

LET us joy and jubilation

In devoutest celebration

Of this sacred feast display;

To exalt the King of Heaven,

Now by all this Church be given

Praise and honor to this day.

On this festal day, as witness

To us, of His glory's brightness

Christ the plainest tokens gave;

For this stor/s due narration

All the grace of His salvation

Fully, freely may we have!

Christ then, mighty God, Bestower

Of all the, and death's O'erthrower,

Very Sun of Righteousness,

Flesh that from a Virgin He deigned to seek,

On this day transfigured on Thabor's peak,

Doth in brightest glory dress.

 *RANSFIGURATION OF OUR LORD*

Blessed fount of good things given!

Such to all that enter heaven

Will the resurrection be.

As the sun shines when it is at its height,

So the God-man's features were shining bright,

As we in the Gospel see.

There His sacred vesture's whiteness

Told of future glory's brightness,

And of God incarnate now.

Over all Thine honor towers

Wondrously, and wondrous powers

Doth, Oh God! Your greatness show!

And, when Christ, God's Word from heaven,

Proof to Peter thus had given.

And the sons of Zebedee,

Of the greatness of His glory,

Lo! they, — Luke attests the story, —

Moses and Elias see.

Matthew gives us information

Of these holding conversation

There with God, God's Son most high:

Very fitting, very holy,

Was such speech, and pleasant truly,

Filled with full felicity.

RANSFIGURATION OF OUR LORD

'Tis a day most celebrated,

Thus by God's voice consecrated;

High distinction has it won!

See the cloud about them gather,

Hear the utterance of the Father;

" This is My Beloved Son! "

Hear ye all God's voice supernal;

It has words of life eternal;

O'er the world His word is king;

Christ, the Lord of all creation,

Saints' bright light and earth's salvation,

Light that lighteth everything!

Christ, the Father's Word from heaven,

Who destroys the stern right given

'Gainst us to our wicked foe,

That dire serpent, who, soul-killing

Poison into Eve instilling.

Wounded all men here below.

We were healed by Christ's death for us,

While His rising did restore us

To new life, and death's power o'er us

Thereby utterly destroy.

Christ it is, our peace supernal,

Lord of heaven and realms infernal,

Whom God thus His voice paternal

To acknowledge did employ.

 *RANSFIGURATION OF OUR LORD*

Those three fathers before stated

By that voice are agitated,

And upon the earth prostrated,

When comes forth its wondrous tone.

Christ at length toward them turning,

They arise, but glances yearning,

Cast around them, thus discerning

Suddenly Christ left alone.

Christ desiring these things hidden.

They to tell them were forbidden.

Till, as life's restorer glorious.

Over life's dread foe victorious,

Life by death should rise again.

Worthy praise the day is truly.

Whereon signs are wrought so holy!

Oh may Christ, his Father's splendor.

Through his mother's blest prayers render

Free from death the sons of men!

Father! Son! to You in heaven,

Holy Spirit! unto You,

Praise and honor due be given.

And supremest majesty! Amen.

T. LAWRENCE

ID the blazing

Conflagration,

Wondering, praising,

Veneration

Pay we Lawrence, laurel-crowned;

Awe-struck bowing,

Venerate him;

Our love showing,

Supplicate him.

As a martyr most renowned. lo

They indict him, —

He denies not;

When they smite him,

He replies but

In the tone soft organs raise:

'Mid flames, playing

Round him, praying.

T. LAWRENCE

He rejoices,

And his voice is

Lifted to his Maker's praise.

As sweet sounds the harp-string wakes

And enchanting music makes,

Which the minstrel's height quill hits,

So the martyr's frame, extended

On the lyre of torture, blended

Strains of faith and hope emits.

Decius! see how

Brave stands he now,

As faith urges

'Neath the scourges,

Threats, and fierce flames mounting high;

Hope internal,

Words supernal,

Consolation,

Exhortation,

Give the man to constancy.

For the treasure which you seeks

With these tortures you bespeaks

For St. La^vrence, not for thee:

He in Christ that wealth is heaping,

Whom, whilst fighting, Christ is keeping

For the palm of victory.

 T. LAWRENCE

Darkness knows the saint's night never,

So that sin should mingle ever

With his pangs through faith too dim:

Nor the blind could he have lightened,

Had no light within him brightened

By its presence all for him.

Our true faith, confest aright,

Shines in Lawrence, pure and bright;

'Neath no bushel placed, its light

In the midst, in all men's sight,

Sets he that it may be seen.

When to bear his cross thus bade,

As God's servant, he is glad,

That he, 'mid the fierce flames laid.

Should a spectacle be made

Both to angels and to men.

Flames he minds not, round him wrapping.

Who from flesh would be escaping,

And abide with Christ for aye:

Neither fears he those men ever.

Who the body kill, but never.

Though they would, the soul can slay.

As the furnace tests by baking

Potters' vessels, harder making

The materials used thereby;

 T. LAWRENCE

So too this man, roast to cinders,

Hard as tiles the fire's heat renders

Through untiring constancy.

For, as the old man decays

In the flame that round him plays.

Firmer yet becomes the new;

While that champion's power receiveth

Thus a rare support, who giveth

Unto God the service due.

Flames up-soaring,

A dew-shower,

Downward pouring,

Through love's power,

And zeal Godward, counts he:

Fire that warms,

Yet nothing harms,

The live fuel

Quenches, cruel

Officer! heaped up by thee!

Scarce one learns

Mustard burns,

Till one use it.

Till one bruise it;

And then sweetest.

When you heatest

It by fire, is incense too:

 *T. LAWRENCE*

So, limbs fastened,

By fire chastened,

'Neath its fury,

Sick and sorry.

Fuller flavor,

Sweeter savor.

Martyrs o'er their virtues throw.

Lawrence, beyond measure glorious!

King sublime, o'er kings victorious!

Who, in righteousness defending,

Counted anguish cheap, contending

Bravely for the King of kings!

Who so many ills o'ercomest,

Looking to Christ's good things promised,

Make us tread down aught distressing,

Make us joy in every blessing,

Through the grace your merit brings! Amen.

ASSUMPTION OF THE BLESSED VIRGIN MARY

GLAD thanks let us Godward carry,

For the Assumption of St, Mary,

Which distinguishes this day:

'Tis a day with gladness mated,

When she was with joy translated

Up to heaven from earth away

O'er angelic choirs uplifted,

She with higher rank was gifted

Than all heaven's own home-born sons.

In His beauty she surveys

There her Son, and there she prays

For all true and faithful ones.

Let us purge out sin's foul traces,

That we thus may in her praises

With hearts purified take part

SSUMPTION OF THE BLESSED

For her ears will listen ever

To our voices, if we never

Discord make 'twixt tongue and heart.

With one heart now let us bless her,

And, while blessing, thus address her,

" Hail, you who such grace does boast!

Hail to you, Christ's mother-maiden!

With your sacred burden laden

By the o'ershading Holy Ghost!

" Holy Virgin! spotless Virgin!

May our voices, upward surging.

Pleasant music to you bear

Bring us help, from heaven descended,

And, when this life's course is ended,

With your Son unite us there! °

" You, from all time pre-elected,

Wast for ages undetected

'Neath the letter of God's law,

Where, that you should'st Christ be bearing.

Prophets of you, truth declaring,

Spoke in types in days of yore.

" Plain the mystery becometh.

When the Word our flesh assumeth,

Of you willing to be born,

SSUMPTION OF THE BLESSED

Who has, in His love most tender,

Been for us a strong defender,

And our race from Satan torn.

" Type of you we hold the gilded

Throne that Solomon derst builded,

Type too Gideon's fleece, to be,

And the bush that never burns

If the mind aright discerns

The old Scriptures' mystery.

" O'er the fleece the dewdrops flowing.

In the bush the bright flame glowing,

Though uninjured both remain,

Point to Christ, who flesh receives,

And who yet your chasteness leaves

Unimpaired by travail-pain.

" From you, as the rod, there springs

Fairest flower, Isaiah sings,

Which shall all the world befriend;

Christ in this fair flower forecasting;

Him, whose virtue, ever lasting.

Ne'er began and ne'er shall end.

" Cistern, whence life's fountain flows!

Lamp, that with warm radiance glows!

'Tis through you that heaven's light throws

Down on us its rays so bright!

SSUMPTION OF THE BLESSED

All the warmth of true love sharing,

Bright with Virgin light appearing,

To the world thine offspring bearing,

The effulgence of God's Light!

" Oh you gate of man's salvation!

Hear us, give us consolation,

And without least hesitation

Call us back whene'er we stray:

From the deep we call you, wailing;

Whilst on this world's ocean sailing.

Save us through your prayer availing

From our furious foe, we pray!

" Jesus, who are our salvation!

For the due commemoration

Of Your mother's worth and station.

With Your grace's free dotation

This our vale to visit deign:

You, who would'st that no man living

Perish, help to us be giving,

That, amid this ocean striving

To live well, at death arriving,

We may fitly rest obtain! " Amen.

## ssumption of the Blessed

VIRGIN, hail! alone the fairest!

Mother, who our Savior barest!

And the name of Sea-Star wearest,

Star that leadeth not astray!

On the sea of this life never

Let us suffer wreck, but ever

To your Savior, to deliver

Those who travel o'er it, pray.

Seethes the sea, the storm-blast blows.

Wild the billows' tumult grows,

Speeds our bark, but, as it goes.

By what crosses is it met!

Siren pleasures' wanton wooing,

Dragon, pirates, dogs, pursuing,

All these threaten death and ruin

To men well-nigh desperate.

SSUMPTION OF THE BLESSED

Now deep down, now up to heaven,

Is our bark by fierce waves driven;

Nods the mast, its full sail riven,

Till the seaman strives no more;

Fast away, such evils tasting,

Is our human life -breath wasting:

Save us, to destruction hasting,

Holy Mother! we implore.

Sprinkled o'er wath heaven's dew-shower,

Still intact your chasteness' flower,

A new flower by new power

Forth from you on earth has come.

Equal to the Sire in Godhead,

In your Virgin frame secluded,

Was the Word for us embodied.

Hidden in your sheltering womb.

You by Him was pre-elected,

By Whom all things are directed.

Who your maiden-mark protected,

When your sacred womb He filled;

Parent of our Savior-brother!

You didst feel nor pain nor other

Sorrow, like to man's first mother,

When you broughtest forth that Child.

SSUMPTION OF THE BLESSED

Mary! for your merits wholly

Hast you been uplifted solely,

O'er the choirs of angels holy,

To a lofty throne above:

Joy is to this day pertaining,

When the heavens you are gaining;

Then on us, below remaining,

Look you with maternal love!

Holy root, that never diest!

Flower, vine, olive, that suppliest

Your own power, and fructifiest

Without foreign graft or seed!

Sunbeams' light and heaven's bright glory! —

' E'en the sun's self pales before thee! —

To Your Son commend our story,

And against strict justice plead.

There, before the King of heaven,

Think of this poor flock sore driven,

Which, transgressing God's law given,

Dares to look for clemency:

For that Judge, Whom love so graces,

Judge deserving endless praises,

'Spite our guilt our hopes high raises,

Crucified upon the tree.

SSUMPTION OF THE BLESSED

Jesus, fruit of womb most holy!

'Mid the storms of this world's folly

Be our way, guide, leader, solely

To the realms of heaven above!

Seize the helm, our vessel steer You,

Off the threatening tempest clear You,

And our vessel onward bear You

To Your pleasant port in love! Amen.

ST. BARTHOLOMEW

COME, let us all with praises now

Bartholomew's rare merits show,

Whose sacred feast-day here below

Makes all our hearts with gladness glow.

He used an hundred times a day

Upon his bended knees to pray;

Nor through the hours of night did he,

Laid prostrate, pray less frequently.

Wherever he was present here

The very devils dumb appear;

When he, Christ's trumpet, soundeth clear,

False gods and idols quake for fear.

He would not Ashtaroth allow

With lies an hapless race to cow:

Nor cheat, nor hurt, them can he now

Nor pity for his victims show.

 T. BARTHOLOMEW

He, worthy of grave punishment,

To \ \ Tithe 'mid fires of hell is sent;

Where by what torments he is rent

From Berith's tale is evident.

Through this Apostle's might alone

The devil's fraud is fully shown;

And, when his cunning craft is known,

No followers more the idol own.

Pseustius exulted, when relieved

From demon's rage, held 'neath control:

And king Polymnius believed,

Because his daughter was made whole.

As 'neath the Apostle's stroke he lies,

The demon from the idol cries;

" From you, my wretched votaries!

I ask no further sacrifice.

" Powerless I am, I now declare,

Who scarce can breathe in torture here:

Before the judgment-day appear,

The punishment by fire I bear! "

He disappeared, as thus he spake.

And his own idol-image brake;

But made none present fear nor quake:

The Cross was there his place to take.

 T. BARTHOLOMEW

With Christ's own mark, the Cross's sign,

An angel's fingers mark the fane.

And thence, through wondrous power divine,

The vexed free absolution gain.

White through baptismal grace we see

India, so dark-hued formerly;

Without a spot, from wrinkle free,

Thus joined to heaven it joys to be.

Their high-priests to Astyages

Then hasten, and, upon their knees,

Demand that he at once will slay

The champion, victor in the fray.

To witness thus for Christ his Lord,

His head he bowed beneath the sword;

So he this day, as victor, shone,

Who India taught and India won.

In constant prayer God's throne before,

For us, Bartholomew! implore,

That we, when this life's course is o'er,

May sing Christ's praise for evermore! Amen.

T. AUGUSTINE

Our tuneful strains let us upraise

That endless feast's delights to praise,

When, since thereon no trouble weighs,

The heart observes true sabbath days;

The rapture of a conscience clear,

That perfumes all those joys sincere,

By which it has rich foretaste here

Of saints' unending glory there,

Where the celestial company

Joys in its home exultingly;

And, giving crowns, their King they see

In all his glorious majesty.

Oh happy land! how great its bliss,

That knows nothing but happiness!

For all the dwellers on that shore

One ceaseless song of praise outpour;

 T. AUGUSTINE

Who those delights' full sweetness feel,

Which not a trace of grief conceal;

'Gainst whom no foeman draws the steel,

And who beneath no tempest reel:

Where one day, clear from cloudlet's haze,

Is better than a thousand days;

Bright with true light's transcendent rays;

Filled with that knowledge of God's ways,

To grasp which human reason fails,

Nor human tongue to tell avails.

Till this mortality shall be

Absorbed in that life's victory;

When God shall all in all appear,

Life, righteousness, and knowledge clear;

Victuals and vesture and whate'er

The pious mind would wish to share!

This in this vale of misery

The sober mind's chief thought should be;

This should it feel, while rest it takes,

This should be with it when it wakes;

How it will in that home, — its days

Of earthly exile past, — fond lays

For ever, crowned, the King to praise

In all His glorious beauty, raise.

T. AUGUSTINE

These praises, sounding loud and clear,

The Church now imitates here;

As, in due order, year by year,

The birthdays of her saints appear;

When, after they have fought their fight,

With worth-won honours they are dight;

The martyr crowned with roses bright;

The virgin clad in robes of white.

They too receive a golden chain,

Who doctrines Catholic maintain:

In which Augustine now does reign.

One of the great King's shining train;

Whose written volumes' full array

Are now the one Faith's strength and stay:

Hence Mother Church avoids the way

Where errors lead mankind astray.

To follow where his steps precede,

And preach the truths He taught indeed.

Mother! may grace your servants lead,

And grant the pure warm faith we need! Amen.

 *T. AUGUSTINE*

FROM the depths of dark obscurest

Comes forth hght, which shines, the purest,

On the earth to-day from heaven:

Once a vessel, truth mistrusting,

Now for honor made, Augustine

To the Church of God was given.

He, the Word of God obeying,

Now believes, once from it straying,

And for grace to baptism comes:

He those errors, once commended,

And in youth with words defended,

Reprobates in written tomes.

Faith confirming, precepts framing,

Those, against Christ's law declaiming,

Slays he with the Word's sharp sword:

Fortunatus' utterance fails.

Manes with Donatus quails,

'Neath such radiant light outpoured.

 *T. AUGUSTINE*

Earth, made void and fast expiring,

But vain doctrines' lore acquiring,

Through the pest of heresy,

To produce much fruit commences,

As the one Faith he dispenses

To its furthest boundary'.

Rules he made for priestly living;

As their pattern, to them giving

The Apostles' company:

Nought their own these priests computed,

But whate'er seemed theirs devoted

To the whole community.

Thus, for many's welfare striving,

Many years in virtue living.

At a good old age arriving,

With his sires he slept at last.

No bequests he left, when dying,

Who, its ownership denying,

Thought his wealth should be supplying

All with whom his lot was cast.

Hail, Confessors' gem bright burning!

Tongue of Christ! heaven's voice of warning!

Trump of life and light of learning!

Prelate high amongst the blest!

ST. AUGUSTINE

May those, Father! who revere you,

'Neath your guidance that life near you

Gain, where joys the truest cheer you

In the Saints' all-glorious rest! Amen.

BEHEADING of ST. JOHN BAPTIST

John, the King of kings' precursor,

John, the new Law's bold rehearser,

Celebrates the Church to-day!

Mother! on so glad a morning

Joy, with praise his name adorning,

And bring forth a votive lay!

Let us keep his birthday rightly.

But rejoice we no less brightly

In the martyrdom he won.

Show, Creation! exultation;

Second is this martyrs station,

In both mark and meed, to none

'Tis not for our fallen nature

To extol each single feature

Of such special sanctity:

Be the tale in sum repeated;

That our love may kindle, heated

With his blessed memory.

EHEADING of ST. JOHN BAPTIST

He, no reed to bend and quiver,

But Truth's pillar, firm for ever,

Never call evil good;

Scribes he strikes at and professors,

Calling all the Law's transgressors

Offspring of a viper's brood.

Herod's sin he censured gravely;

Bound by him, he bore up bravely.

In a prison kept secure:

Pains unjust the just endureth,

Who such filthiness abhorreth

In the king and paramour,

Tyrant power against him burneth:

Whence John greater honor earneth,

And the tyrant torments dure:

Help to wisdom folly gives,

Since the just, while here he lives,

By the impious is made pure.

At his birthday-feast at even

Orders by the king are given,

That the head of John be brought.

She who danced that head receiveth

From the officer, and giveth

To her mother what she sought.

*EHEADING of ST. JOHN BAPTIST*

Christ's increase the Cross foreshoweth,

But, that less the Baptist groweth,

His beheading shadows forth.

Precious, if the life preceding

Glory o'er that life were shedding,

Is the righteous' death on earth.

Christ! the better to adore You

Through the Baptist sent before You,

We this feast-day celebrate:

Out of death's dark valley lead us

Thither, where his steps precede us,

And our path to life make straight! Amen

T. GILES

LET us joy with exultation,

And, exulting, celebration

Make to-day of Giles's rites,

Who, o'er things of earth victorious,

Seeks those joys of all most glorious,

And a crown in heavenly heights!

He, for piety most noted,

Full of holiness devoted,

Scion of a regal race.

Soon to be God's holy temple,

And earth's very bright example,

Was begotten of God's grace.

In his youth's first early flower,

What in riper age his power

Would be, he, through grace, foreshowed

Clothing to a beggar giving,

Medicine too, his health reviving.

He on him, long sick, bestowed.

 T. GILES

When his parents died, o'erflowing

With the praise due to well-doing,

Selling all, with open hand

Needy strangers he endows,

And, himself a pauper, goes,

Exiled, from his native land.

Sailors, tempest-tost and wearied,

To the port they seek are carried.

Rescued by his earnest prayer:

To a widow he restores

Whole her child, while she implores

A physician in despair.

Barrenness away is chased,

By fertility replaced.

And a plenteous harvest comes:

Sick men with new health are filled,

Dire diseases thence expelled,

ausing joy in mournful homes.

To a bare and barren waste.

Sore athirst, he then made haste,

To escape from man's abode.

Christ Himself was present there, —

Since but scanty was the fare, —

To provide His servant's food;

 T. GILES

Lest of hunger he should die,

A wild animal drew nigh

To sustain the man of God.

Hidden thus he fain would be,

But the royal family

Of his place of hiding hear:

Through his nurse discovered, there

At the monarch's earnest prayer

He a monastery near, —

Where he many a warrior bold.

In the cause of Christ enrolled,

By his side encamped, — does rear.

Through this monarch's prayer, whoever

Prays to Giles devoutly never, —

France is witness, — prays in vain;

For, when for the king he prays

On whose mind a dark deed weighs,

He his pardon does obtain.

To receive those laurels soon

By his earthly triumphs won,

Has this saint to heaven gone,

Whom the host about God's throne

To those mansions, where alone

Peace and glory are, led on.

# T. GILES

Giles's feast then venerate we,

Venerating, consecrate we

In perpetual memory!

Humbly now let us entreat him,

And, entreating, supplicate him,

That true joys our portion be.

Where in bliss that ends never

We may Alleluias ever

With the Saints sing joyfully! Amen.

T. GILES

LOVING hymns, Precentor! bringing,

This Confessor's praise be singing!

To extol him, Choir! before us

Sing this sweet and festive chorus!

Dear to God through faith devoted,

Of a race in this world noted,

Earthly pomps he scorned still, striving

Pure in God's sight to be living.

In his years of boyhood even

Such great parts to him were given,

That the teacher soon he turned

E'en of teachers the most learned.

He, within, with warm love glows,

And, without, bright virtues shows;

Love's strong heat, within residing,

Shines without, all others guiding.

 T. GILES

To one sick his robe he sends,

And his sickness straightway ends;

Thus at once, through power from heaven,

Clothes and health by him are given.

All his riches he surrendered,

And to Christ, as offerings, tendered:

Needy he became to feed them

With his goods, who most did need them.

Whilst he on the poor thus spends,

Greater wealth to him Christ sends;

Off for Christ things temporal casting,

He obtains those everlasting.

Of the crime a monarch fears

To confess to him he hears;

Christ to him the facts revealing

Of the monarch's evil dealing.

For whilst, at the altar waiting,

He a mass was celebrating,

From above a scroll descended,

Telling how the king offended.

Having thus dread insight given

To a deed abhorred of heaven.

Now in humble prayer he boweth

For the king whose crime he knoweth.

 *T. GILES*

Help he from a hind receiveth,

Which in gratitude she giveth;

Moved by God, her succor tendering,

As it were thanks to him rendering.

Far more deeds with marvel glowing

Might be found of this Saint's doing,

Showing us to demonstration

How illustrious is his station.

To this choir his help be given,

That they evermore in heaven,

Gazing on the King eternal,

Glory with the Saints supernal!   Amen.

NATIVITY of the BLESSED VIRGIN

HAIL to you, our Savior's mother!

Vessel, honored o'er all other!

Chosen vessel of God's grace!

Vessel, known before creation!

Noble vessel, whose formation

'Neath the All-wise hand took place!

Hail, the world's own mother holy!

Sprung from thorns, but thornless throughly!

Flower a thornbrake's glory born!

We the thornbrake are, surrounded

With sin's thorns, and by them wounded,

But you are without a thorn.

Closed gate! fount through gardens pouring!

Storehouse, precious spikenard storing!

Store of unguents sweet to smell!

*ATIVITY of the BLESSED VIRGIN*

Cinnamon's sweet-scented reed,

Incense, balsam, myrrh, indeed

You in fragrance do excel!

Hail, fair type of maiden grace;

Mediatrix of man's race!

Of salvation brought to bed!

Continence's myrtle-tree!

Rose of love and clemency!

Nard whence sweetest scents are shed!

Lowliest of valleys thou,

Soil that never felt the plough,

Which to God himself gave birth!

Meadow-flower! lily fair!

Which the valley, peerless, bare!

Christ of you was born on earth!

Oh you paradise in heaven!

Lebanon no axe has riven,

Breathing sweetness all around!

Virgin whiteness, beauty's brightness,

Finest flavours, sweetest savors,

Plenteously in you abound!

You the wise king's throne appearest.

Which, in shape and substance, fairest,

'Mongst all thrones has ever been:

ATIVITY of the BLESSED VIRGIN

Chastity in ivory's whiteness,

Charity in red gold's brightness,

Shadowed forth, therein are seen.

Peerless is the palm you bearest,

Peerless you on earth appearest,

And in heaven amongst the blest:

As the praise of all man's race,

You peculiar virtues grace,

Given to you above the rest.

As the sun outshines the moon,

And the moon each twinkling star,

Mary is than every one

Of God's creatures worthier far!

Light, that no eclipse can know,

Is her virgin chastity;

Heat, which ne'er will cease to glow,

Her love's deathless constancy!

{As the venerable Adam was saluting the Blessed Virgin Mary in the following stanza, he was himself in return saluted and thanked by her.)

Mother of fair love, we name thee!

Famed triclinium we proclaim thee,

Which the Trinity all share;

ATIVITY of the BLESSED VIRGIN

Though you does a special dwelling

For the majesty excelling

Of the Incarnate Word prepare!

Mary, Star o'er ocean glowing!

Rival none in honor knowing!

Foremost in precedence going

'Mongst all ranks around God's throne!

Placed in highest heaven, commend us

To thine Offspring to befriend us,

And from fear of foes defend us,

Lest by guile we be o'erthrovvn.

Safe, in battle-line extended,

May we be, by you defended;

May foes' force and shrewdness blended

Bow before your virtues splendid,

And their craft 'neath your foresight.

Christ the Word, God's generation!

Guard Your mother's congregation;

Pardon guilt, grant free salvation.

And with the illumination

Of Your glory make us bright! Amen.

ATIVITY *of the BLESSED VIRGIN*

Dawns a day for adoration,

Day, when in glad jubilation

Songs enlightened hearts should raise!

This day's joyous light another

Feast-day brings round of God's mother,

Dedicated to her praise!

Voice! now keep you

Joyful measure;

Heart! now leap you,

Filled with pleasure,

That your praise effective be!

Let God's glory

So be lauded,

That the story

Be applauded

Of his mother's dignity!

Great in splendor

Of her station

ATIVITY of the BLESSED VIRGIN

Very tender

In compassion,

Sorrowful is she by name;

Honour-laden,

As child-bearing

Still a maiden

Pure appearing,

Bright in heaven's height shines her fame!

As of old the bush to Moses

Seems in flames, yet never loses

Aught, by burning, of its green;

So by spiritual graces,

Not by conjugal embraces,

Has a maid God's mother been.

She is that sealed fount, ne'er drying,

That walled garden, fructifying

By the good seed in it sown:

She is that close-fastened portal,

Shut by God 'gainst every mortal

For some secret cause unknown All

She that fleece is, which invites

Dew; that rich field that delights

With sweet scents all ends of earth:

She that rod is, blossoms bearing,

Soil for all, true faith declaring.

To a Savior giving birth.

*ATIVITY of the BLESSED VIRGIN*

She is titled, for example,

"Mountain," "Castle," "Hall," and "Temple,"

"Bridal Chamber," "Citadel":

To her now has there been given,

Of sublimest names in heaven,

That which does the rest excel.

Whose petitions vices quell,

Whose name sorrow does dispel.

Whose rare scents like lilies smell,

Whose sweet lips by far excel

Honey's nectar in delight.

Daintier than the wine-cup's flow.

Whiter than the driven snow,

Fresher than rose, washed but now,

Brighter with the true Sun's glow

Than the pale moon's orb by night.

Queen o'er glorious

Realms supernal,

And victorious

O'er infernal!

All-availing

Path to heaven.

Whence unfailing

Faith's ne'er driven!

ATIVITY of the BLESSED VIRGIN

All those falling

From you wholly,

Now recalling

From their folly,

With your own once more unite!

Oh good Mother,

Whom we pray to!

Grant our other

Prayers to-day too;

Sinners, straying.

Ne'er so spurn your, As from praying

Hearts to turn now:

Sinners, wholly

Self-diffiding,

With those, truly

Your abiding,

Lead into your dear Son's sight! Amen.

*ATIVITY of the BLESSED VIRGIN*

HAIL, Oh mother of Christ Jesus!

Who from heaven that Son so precious

Didst conceive uncarnally!

Pure from contact with aught human,

You conceived, who, as woman,

Should'st with joy Joy's parent be!

You have borne a medicine, given

Not of man, but sprung from heaven,

To an age in swift decay:

All the world in great prostration,

All the world in tribulation.

All the world in peril, lay.

This world's sin was this world's weakness.

And there is no direr sickness,

None so deadly at the last.

ATIVITY *of the* BLESSED VIRGIN

Satan was in full possession,

Since down steeps of foul transgression

All the world was gliding fast.

Not yet had that seed appeared,

Which God's promise had declared

From the first to us should come;

Seed with woman as its source,

Without carnal intercourse,

Sprung from mother's spotless womb.

Of a woman choice was made,

Whom that serpent old essayed

In the heel to wound and tear:

But she, wise, and valiant too,

Made no compact with the foe,

Of his deadly sting aware.

She, with whose flesh to be blended

God's Son's glory condescended,

Bruised the subtle serpent's head:

Woman, though but weak and frail.

Doth to crush hell's power avail,

Woman, easily misled!

Virgin, who in glory shinest!

Precious beyond gold the finest!

Sweeter far than lilies! hail!

ATIVITY of the BLESSED VIRGIN

Meadows' fairness yields before thee;

Flowers', gems', beauty, with the glory

Of proud Lebanon's forests, pale

To your Son, you Star of Ocean!

Mary! ever with devotion

For your fellow-servants pray;

Since temptations are unending,

Endless are our sobs heart-rending,

And our sighs from day to day.

Oh may our prayers, our sighs, our tears.

With pity touch thine heart within;

And, by the power your virtue bears.

Do you restrain what prompts to sin.

Let carnal ways, so smooth and bright.

The means to misdeeds ne'er be made:

Nor this world's empty joys delight,

With Christ's free grace at hand to aid! Amen.

The End

Credits:

CHISWICK PRESS:

C. WHITTINGHAM AND CO. TOOKS COURT,

CHANCERY LANE. 526146

1881

Visit us at your local bookstore on the web at our web site:

http://revelationinsight.tripod.com/

E-Mail: Mystic@orthodox.com

Visit us at your local bookstore on the web at our web site

FREE BOOK offer for visiting our website: "His Daily Bread"

All works _always_ at least % off retail, through our store

Works of the "Catholic Classics" Series

Volumes 1-

1st segment

Explanation of the Rule of St Augustine OSA	Hugh of St. Victor
Treatise of the Spiritual Life Books 1-3	Bishop Morozzo O.Cist
Imitation of Christ	Thomas a' Kempis

2nd segment

Little Book of Wisdom   Henry Suso O.P.

Note: vol. 2-4 are fraternal twins writings

Works of the "Desert Fathers" Series

Volumes 1-4

1st segment

Wisdom of the Desert   James O' Hanney

Desert Fathers Books 1 & 2   Countess Hahn-Hahn

Evigarius Essentials   Evigarius

2nd segment

Works for the Master

"Philosopher's Palate" Series

Vol. 1-4

1st segment

Divine Names   Pseudo Dionysius

First Principle   Duns Scotus OFM

Boethius   Consolation of Philosophy

Pesenes   Paschal

Works for the Journeyman

"Great Christian Mystical Writings"

Volumes 1-

1st segment

Ascent of Mount Carmel	St. John of the Cross
Dark Night of the Soul	St. John of the Cross
A Cell of Knowledge	Anonymous
Divine Consolation	Angelina Foligno OFM

2nd segment

A Cloud of Unknowing   Walter Hilton

"The Contemplative" Series

Volumes 1-3

1st segment

Ladder of Perfection	Walter Hilton OSA
Selection of Hugh of St Victor OSA	Hugh of St Victor
Third Spiritual Alphabet	Francisco de Osuna OFM

Works for the Apprentice

The Initial Series

"Pilgrim's Pantry"

Volumes 1-

1st segment

The Kneeling Christian	Anonymous
Passion of Christ	Bro Smith SGS
Way of Perfection	Teresa of Avila
Augustine Essentials	Augustine

2nd segment

Ascent of the Pilgrim   J. Boheme, H. Scougal, F.B. Meyer

Research Essentials" Series

Volumes 1-4

1st segment

Medieval to Modern English Dictionary	R /I Publishing Staff
Contemplative Life	St. Bruno
Ecclesiastical History	Bede OSB
Church Creeds	Various

2nd segment

Greek to English Dictionary   James Strong

"The Monastic Series"

Volumes 1-6

1st segment

A Short Overview of Monasticism	Alfred Wishart
Monasticism from Egypt to the 4th Cent	W. Mackean

2nd segment

A Monk's Topical Bible in 4 Books.

The Thomas Aquinas Library

Volumes 1-6

1st segment

The Companion to the Summa   (in 4 vols.)   Walter Farrell O.P.

2nd segment

Contra Gentiles   Thomas
Aquinas O.P.

Women of Faith Series

Volumes 1-3

1st segment

OCD

	Interior Castle	Teresa of Avila
	The Dolorious Passion	Catherine Emmerich OSA
	Dialogues	Catherine of Sienna
	Showings	Julian of Norwich

Spiritual Poetry & Literature Series

Volumes 1-3

1st segment

Liturgical Poetry   Adam of St Victor OSA

French Enlightenment Series

Volumes 1-2

1st segment

Fenelon's Finest	Francis de Fenelon
Selections	Francis de Sales

All these works may be purchased through us directly or from your local bookstore.

Each series will comprise of 12 volumes each.

Visit us at your local bookstore on the web at our web site

FREE BOOK offer for visiting our website:

"His Daily Bread"

All works <u>always</u> at least % off retail through our store

Free shipping within the USA

http://revelationinsight.tripod.com/

E-Books in

Kindle

www.ingramcontent.com/pod-product-compliance
Lightning Source LLC
Chambersburg PA
CBHW030233170426
43201CB00006B/203